Sin and Salvation in the World Religions

A SHORT INTRODUCTION

Sin and Salvation in the World Religions

A SHORT INTRODUCTION

Harold Coward

ONEWORLD
OXFORD

SIN AND SALVATION IN THE WORLD RELIGIONS:
A SHORT INTRODUCTION

Oneworld Publications
(Sales and Editorial)
185 Banbury Road
Oxford OX2 7AR
England
www.oneworld-publications.com

ISBN 1–85168–319–4

Cover design by Design Deluxe, Bath
Cover image © the art archive/Turkish and Islamic Arts Museum, Istanbul.
Photographer: Dagli Orti (A.)
Typeset by LaserScript Limited, Mitcham, UK
Printed and bound in Spain by Book Print S.L.

To my sisters
Beverley and Bernice

Contents

Acknowledgments

I wish to thank Novin Doostdar of Oneworld for encouraging me to write this book. June Thomson gave me valuable assistance in library research and Vicki Simmons in preparation of the manuscript. Thanks are due to several colleagues who kindly read draft chapters and offered suggestions for revision: Elizer Segal, Andrew Rippin, Earl Waugh, Roger Hutchinson, Anatanand Rambachan, David Loy, and Robert Florida. Helpful suggestions were also received from Roland Miller, Hanna Kassis, and Fred Denny.

To make this volume as accessible as possible to readers who do not know the sacred languages, diacriticals have been omitted from Hebrew, Arabic, and Sanskrit words.

1

Introduction

At the still point of the turning world. Neither flesh nor
  fleshless;
Neither from nor towards; at the still point, there the dance is,
But neither arrest nor movement. And do not call it fixity,
Where past and future are gathered.

T. S. ELIOT, "Burnt Norton"[1]

Reading these lines as a young university undergraduate
awakened within me a fondness for religious speculation about
the "still point of the turning world" – the still point from
which the pattern of the universe can be seen. Some years later,
while studying Hindu and Buddhist philosophy, speculation on
the "still point" was revived in a debate over its nature – stasis
or change. For the Hindu the "still point" is consciousness
shorn of its changing mental states – the mind calmed until it
becomes still like an unrippled mountain lake that perfectly
reflects its surroundings. For the Buddhist, however, the "still
point" that is left when thought ceases is just the steady flow of
consciousness, like a clear constantly moving mountain stream
in which the world is perfectly reflected. The Hindu–Buddhist
debate over the nature of the "still point" as unchanging versus
changing consciousness is revisited in the contemporary

Western *logos* versus deconstruction argument. The Eastern debate has gone on since the time of the Buddha (*c.* 560 B.C.E.), and the contemporary Western argument can be traced back, in its seed form, to Athens versus Jerusalem. In human religious experience the quest for the "still point," and the pattern of the universe it reveals, is seen in the search for salvation within the world's religious traditions.

As a young boy growing up in the foothills of the Canadian Rocky Mountains, I was imprinted early with the silent splendor of nature. The quiet drama of a brilliantly painted sunrise on prairie sky, broken by the clear sweet sound of the meadow lark, was transcended only by the numinous experience of climbing to the top of a mountain and being overwhelmed by feelings of insignificance and elation in the vastness of the universe. There one's sinful failings and human limitations seemed to be swallowed up in something larger. From that mountaintop perspective one does indeed seem to be at "the still point of the turning world." Patterns can be sensed, but not explicitly. There is a strong mystical tendency towards stillness. Time is not evaded, but past and future are gathered into the present. There is an aesthetic perception of truth which cannot be conceptually expressed and which can only be pointed to by poets, painters, and musicians. Such experiences encapsulate the essence of religion and its search for release from human limitations.

The external mystery of nature was more than matched in my early inner experience of the "still point" of thought. I remember one day as a young child of perhaps five or six years being sent to my room by mother for an afternoon nap. Lying there in silence, my mind was suddenly overwhelmed with questions: "Why?" "Why am I here?" "What is the meaning of it all?" Later, as a young man, I resonated strongly with Paul when he cried out in Romans 7: "I do not what I want, but I do the very thing I hate ... Wretched man that I am. Who will rescue me from this body of death?" It is these questions,

questions that we all experience, that the religions of the world seek to answer through their understandings of "Sin and Salvation." In their answers they each offer a vision of the universal pattern that one senses must be there in one's mountaintop "still point" experiences. This book looks at the sometimes quite different answers offered by the religious traditions of Judaism, Christianity, Islam, Hinduism, and Buddhism.

In presenting the thinking of each religious tradition on "sin and salvation," I have tried to follow a common approach. Each chapter begins with a consideration of "The Human Condition," the starting point from which we begin our search for salvation. This is followed by an analysis of how the scripture of that religious tradition views sin and salvation. Then some of the major thinkers or schools of thought are surveyed for their further development of the scriptural ideas. Examples from recent scholars within the tradition are included. Where appropriate a final section examines views of life after death in relation to sin and salvation.

"Salvation" is a term which arises most clearly in the Christian tradition – the idea that God's love through Jesus Christ will save humans from their sinful state. However, other religions have parallel concepts. Rather than salvation, Jews speak of "redemption" for individuals, for Israel and indeed for all nations. In Islam the closest parallel is found in the term *najat* which means "escape or deliverance from the fires of hell to the pleasures of paradise by following God's guidance." In Judaism, Christianity, and Islam the human condition from which we all begin is one of sin or disobedience to God, and it is from that state that we need to be saved. When we turn to Hinduism and Buddhism, however, it is human ignorance rather than sin that is our baseline human experience. Our ignorance traps us in a seemingly unending series of lives – of birth, aging, sickness, and death repeated over and over. This apparently endless series of suffering, death, and rebirth is the human condition that leads one to long for "release from rebirth" – the Hindu and Buddhist functional parallel to the idea of salvation. "Release" for Hindus is referred to as *moksa*, while Buddhists call it *nirvana*.

In his classic work, *The Varieties of Religious Experience*,[2] the psychologist William James suggests that we humans innately seek for a wider sense of ourselves through which saving experiences come. This "wider self," says James, might well be the door that the divine uses to enter into the lives of humans here on earth.[3] In the chapters that follow we are introduced to different perceptions of the divine, of our human condition, and of the "wider sense of self" through which salvation may come. In the history of the human search for salvation we find not only differences between religions but also a great variety of understandings within each tradition. What is common, however, is the basic insight found in all the religious traditions "that this world is not a place in which we are hopelessly lost, that evil or illusory as the world may be, and sinful or ignorant as we are, there is a way, a path, that leads from darkness to light, from lostness to salvation."[4]

2

Judaism

Rather than "salvation," Jews speak of redemption for individuals, for Israel, and indeed for all the nations. For Jews God is understood in three ways: as creator, revealer, and redeemer. Morning and evening the daily prayer, the *Shema*, praises God as the creator of the world. Of the daily blessings to be said, the second speaks of how God has revealed his plan for creation through the Torah, the scripture given through Moses to his people Israel. As Neusner puts it, "The covenant made at Sinai, a contract on Israel's side to do and hear the Torah, on God's side to be the God of Israel – that covenant is evoked by natural events, then confirmed by the deeds and devotion of men."[1] And this is where the problem occurs, for as individuals and as a group the people of Israel inevitably seem to fall short of what God, in the covenant agreement, asks of them. It is from this failure that humans need to be redeemed. It is this third way of experiencing God as redeemer that concludes the daily prayers of the pious Jew:

> You are our King and our father's King
> Our redeemer and our father's redeemer.
> You are our creator . . .
> You have ever been our redeemer and deliverer
> There can be no God but You.

The prayer recounts how God rescued the forefathers from bondage in Egypt, how Moses and the redeemed people of Israel at Sinai sang a new song to the Lord, and how God will humble the proud, raise the lowly and help the needy. The prayer concludes by calling on God:

> Fulfill your promise to deliver Judah and Israel.
> Our redeemer is the Holy One of Israel,
> The Lord of hosts is his name.
> Praised are You, O Lord, redeemer of Israel.[2]

For the people of Israel, God's redeeming activity is in the past in Egypt, promised in Torah for the future, and active in the present wherever the proud are humbled and the lowly raised up. Neusner summarizes, "Just as creation is not only in the beginning, but happens every day morning and night, so redemption is not only at the Red Sea, but every day, in humble events. Just as revelation was not at Sinai alone, but takes place whenever man studies Torah, whenever God opens man's heart to the commandments, so redemption and creation are daily events."[3] As the *Shema* is said each day, God's creating, revealing, and redeeming activities are recounted, evoked, and celebrated. From this threefold worldview of God as "creator," "revealer," and "redeemer," we will focus, in this chapter, on the third – the Jewish understanding of redemption. First we will examine the Jewish conception of the human condition in which we find ourselves and from which we need to be redeemed. Second, we will trace the evolution of the Jewish conception of redemption from the earliest scriptures of the Torah, the Pentateuch, through the prophets, the Sages of the Oral Torah, medieval philosophy, the mystics of the Kabbalah, and modern thinkers such as Buber, Heschel, and Rosenzweig. Finally there is a description of the way in which Jewish ideas of the resurrection of the body and the afterlife factor in to thinking about redemption.

THE HUMAN CONDITION – LIFE UNDER TORAH

From the Jewish perspective each person is trapped between what the Torah or scripture tells us to do and what we are actually able to achieve. Just as those in the past who lived in bondage in Egypt disobeyed their promises to God and yet were still delivered from their failures by God, so also, when we fail today, it is God who stands by us and redeems us. And when God's will is done by the people of Israel, then all people will recognize that the unique destiny of Israel is intended for everyone – that Israel's hope for redemption is ultimately the hope of everyone (the message of prophets like Jeremiah, Isaiah, and Ezekiel).

The prophets emphasized that what the Torah required from people was not just religious observance but also moral behaviour – indeed that both morality and religion form a unity in the teaching of the Pentateuch as they do in the nature of God. The prophets condemned not only idolatry but also injustice and oppression in any form, especially poverty resulting from social evil. Anyone more favored in personal attainments or material wealth has a greater responsibility to help others. As the prophet Jeremiah puts it, "Let not the wise man glory in his wisdom, neither let the mighty man glory in his might, neither let the rich man glory in his riches. But let him that glorieth glory in this, that he understandeth and knoweth Me, that I am the Lord who exercise mercy, justice and righteousness in the earth" (Jer. 9:23–24). God is active in history, in daily life, and calls people, through Torah, to work with God in doing away with poverty and injustice. The prophets offer a vision of world harmony and unity in which all people will reverence the one God. The culmination of this vision was called "the day of the Lord" and symbolized the rule of universal righteousness on earth.[4] It would come to Israel, said Jeremiah, as a new covenant that would enforce the covenant made with Israel at Sinai in the giving of the Torah.

While the Torah had communicated an understanding of God's wishes, the people of Israel had continued to act in deceitful and stubborn ways. To overcome this failure, the new covenant would not depend on recalling God's saving of the Israelites in the past. Now, through this new covenant, "the Torah of Sinai would be engraved in the very heart of the people and operate with a power of instinctive and instantaneous response to the demands of God ... Thus shall the knowledge of God become the common possession of all Israel and through Israel all the nations of the world."[5] All people will worship and serve God – redemption will be universal.

The purpose of this new covenant is to replace our ordinary life dominated by the senses – lust, greed, violence, and passion – with a true living under Torah which would create a new social order dominated by a realized knowledge of the Lord. The prophet Ezekiel taught that this new earth must begin with the individual. One should not rely on the priests, Temple, or sacrifices to save the whole of Israel. Rather, each person must choose to be delivered from sin and through confession and service to others create a new spirit within. Then God will respond: "A new heart also, I will give you, a new spirit I will put within you" (Ezek. 36:26). No longer subject to fate, through personal relationship with God the individual is reconciled and redeemed from sin.

As we have seen the fundamental basis of human life for all Jews is that it is to be lived under Torah – God's revelation in the Bible and in subsequent oral teachings. "Torah is understood as law that obligates Israel (and to a lesser extent all humanity) to a pattern of behaviour and a communal relationship with God (the covenant)."[6] Disorder in life comes from failure to remain faithful to the covenant with God. By following the Torah, however, Israel can live in harmony with God and with the universe in the midst of the tensions of daily life. Ben Sirach, a Jewish writer living in Jerusalem about 180 B.C.E., summarizes the human condition in relation to God as follows:

> It was he who made man in the beginning,
> and left him in the hand of his own deliberation.
> If you choose, you can keep the commandments,
> and faithfulness is to do [God's] good will...
> Before each person are life and death,
> and whichever one chooses will be given.[7]

In creating the universe God made humans with free choice, to work with God by fostering harmony, or to go against God by pursuing selfish sinful ways. By choosing faithfulness to God, one finds life; by choosing sin one fosters disorder and death. Rabbinic Judaism, which arose in the first century C.E. and continues right up to the present, further elaborates the Jewish understanding of the human condition. The Rabbinic commentators are especially concerned with the human tendency toward evil which leads to sin. As creator, God is seen to have some responsibility in this regard. Yet the commentators fully embrace human freedom and the responsibility for sin even as they lament conflicts between good and evil in human life. The complexity of the Rabbinic analysis is seen in Tractate Berakot 9:5:

> A person is bound to bless [God] for the evil even as he blesses for the good, as scripture says, "You shall love the Lord your God with all your heart and with all your soul and with all your strength" (Deuteronomy 6:5). "With all your heart" means with both your impulses, with the good impulse and the evil impulse; "with all your soul" means even if [God] takes away your soul; "with all your strength" means with all your wealth. Another explanation: "with all your strength" means with whatever measure [God] measures out to you, give thanks to him greatly.[8]

Here the human condition is compressed into three experiences: (1) humans experience good and evil in life because the human heart (the seat of thought, emotion, and will) is divided between tendencies to good and evil; (2) evil constantly threatens the soul (the principle of life) with death; and (3) to maintain life and resist evil and temptation requires more than human resources, namely strength from God for redemption. Jews in the modern period, especially after the Holocaust, have struggled with the problem of how to understand suffering and evil in a world created and ordered by God. For a modern Jew, the human condition involves "wrestling with God in an imperfect world" but still with a hope for ultimate redemption.[9]

EVOLUTION OF THE JEWISH CONCEPT OF REDEMPTION

In the Torah

In the Hebrew Bible the word "redeemer" and its related terms "redeem" and "redemption" are derived from two Hebrew roots, *pdh* and *g'l*. *Pdh* comes originally from commercial law and refers to a person or animal which is released in return for a financial payment or an acceptable replacement. *G'l* comes from family law and concerns the Israelite view that the solidarity of the clan or extended family must be maintained – for example, one is to redeem one's clansman who has been reduced to poverty by slavery (Lev. 25:47ff.) or one supports the widow of one's next of kin (Ruth 4:4ff.). In addition to these usages in ordinary human affairs, these two terms were also applied to divine activities, but with a slight shift in emphasis. *Pdh* takes on the general meaning of "deliverer" but does not include the "payment of an equivalent" idea since, as the creator of the universe, God already owns everything. God's purpose is not to retain the right of possession but to liberate people (both individuals and groups) from bondage, oppression, and death. In Deuteronomy, *pdh* characterizes God's acts at the time of the Exodus as redemptive (e.g. Deut. 9:26). Prophets such as Jeremiah and Isaiah extend this idea to include eschatological redemption and the Psalmists (e.g. Ps. 130:8) to deliverance from sins. *G'l*, when referring to God, loses its juridical connection and comes to mean "deliverer." In

Isaiah 54:8, for example, God is described as taking the initiative just because of his boundless love and passionate concern for justice.[10]

The Sages of the Oral Law

When one turns to the Sages or the teachers of the Oral Law, Urbach notes that their thinking regarding redemption is closely linked to the Pentateuch, to the prophets and to the visions of the book of Daniel.[11] Yet the Sages (authors of the Mishna, Talmud, and later writings) offer an independent approach to the concept in a variety of views. This variety stems from diverse uses of the term *ga'al* (to redeem) and *ge'ula* (redemption), along with various terms (e.g. "end of the days," "end," "days of the Messiah," "resurrection of the dead," "the world to come," "the future to come," and "the new world") associated with "redemption."[12] The changing of these ideas into some aspect of redemption is triggered by the experience of catastrophes such as the exile of Israel to Babylon (*c.* 598–515 B.C.E.) or the destruction of the Second Temple by the Romans (70 C.E.). In the prophets we find teachings regarding the "End" linked to the new revelation, the new covenant, and the redemption of the people of Israel from their bondage to other nations. And this is seen to be important not only for Israel but for the future of the whole world. Here too the image of a Messiah or redeemer is evoked as the saviour of Israel from the other nations and the bringer of righteousness (e.g. Is. 11:1–10). The prophets reinforce the teaching that redemption is dependent on repentance and good deeds. Unlike Christianity, however, the role of the Messiah in the process of redemption "is no different from those of Moses and other redeemers in the past; he is merely an instrument in the hands of God."[13]

While the Hebrew Bible uses both *padah* and *ga'al* for redemption, the Sages of the Talmud use *padah* for "ransom" and *ga'al* for redemption. In their view no special grace is required from God. All that is required by individuals, or the people of Israel, is the correct choosing and effort of humans under the guidance of Torah. However there is a view that the final redemption would be the act of God, and would be eternal. But again there are differences over whether Gentiles who convert will be included. Some suggest that proselytes will not be included while others talk of the redemption of Israel as bringing with it the redemption of the whole world.[14]

According to Urbach's analysis of the writings of the Sages, as long as the Temple stood and self-rule in some form occurred in Judea, national-Messianic hopes were not expressed in terms of redemption.[15] In the prayers and writings of the period, there is no sense of catastrophe present. The Temple is built and the sons of Zadok, the High Priest, preside in it as they should. Although the return of all Jews from the diaspora has yet to be completed, hopes for the future are of a routine and realistic nature with no reference to the "End." The thinking of the time is realistic, concerned with Israel's national sovereignty and prosperity. However, with the beginning of the Hasmonean era (142–63 B.C.E.), the idea of redemption resurfaced on coins, but with reference to redemption of Zion (the nation) rather than to the "End-time." Redemption was to be from national troubles. The Sages of the period recognized the leadership of the Hasmoneans and of Herod in the monarchy, the priesthood, and the Temple. Herod, especially, was praised for his work in rebuilding the Temple. The focus of the Sages was on the teaching of the Torah, interpretation of scripture, and instruction of the people regarding faith in Divine Providence, in reward and punishment and in the resurrection of the dead.[16] Little attention is paid to the prophetic visions or Messianic promises of redemption. With disintegration of the Hasmonean rule in 63 B.C.E. over the wars between the brothers Aristobus and Hyrcanus, and the capture of Jerusalem by Pompey, Messianic thinking reappears. The work called the

Messianic Psalm, says Urbach, rejects the monarchy of the Hasmoneans and calls upon God to establish a new king, a Messiah who is a son of David. He will be a redeemer of the land and nation as well as a cosmic redeemer, who promises the kingdom of the Lord upon earth. This document is also unique in what it omits – there is no mention of reward or punishment in the world to come, resurrection of the dead, or catastrophic scenes. Redemption, right up until the Second Temple destruction is understood by the Sages as having to do with the enlargement of Jewish independence. Messianic expectations were not considered to be of immediate or practical significance.[17] But with the destruction of the Second Temple by the Romans in 70 C.E. a great change occurs in the concept of redemption. The immediate response from many was to attempt to rebuild the Temple and proclaim that the Messiah would soon come. But, notes Urbach, Rabbis of the day such as Johanan b. Zakkai began immediately "reconstructing the life of Torah and precept, and although he did this in the hope that the Sanctuary would be rebuilt and the people redeemed, he realized that these things could not happen in the near future."[18]

Following the destruction of the Temple, the Sages' discussion of redemption introduces an emphasis on repentance. Rabbi Eliezer b. Hycranus said, "If Israel repent they will be redeemed, but if not, they will not be redeemed."[19] Urbach comments that this text implies a religious–national redemption which would restore Israel to its former glory, including renewal of national freedom, rebuilding the Temple as a prerequisite to perfecting the world under the rule of God, and the fulfillment of the promises of the prophets about the last days.[20] Repentance comes first, then redemption. Rabbi Joshua adds that should Israel not repent, the Messiah will come and bring Israel back to the right path, namely the path of repentance, for it is inconceivable that Israel will not be redeemed. This addition allows for speculation as to when the Messiah will come and as to what catastrophic events may accompany the End. Rabbi Eliezer differs from Rabbi Joshua in that he does not rely on catastrophic events to bring the people of Israel to repentance. When asked, "What shall a man do to save himself from the throes of the Messiah's coming?" Rabbi Eliezer replied, "Let him occupy himself with the study of the Torah and with the practice of benevolence."[21] Repentance in this fashion brings redemption without having to wait for the intervention of the Messiah or the coming of the End time. Rabbi Akiba, a student of Rabbi Joshua, adopted his teacher's view in which the repentance and redemption of Israel are linked to the Messiah and the End time. But Rabbi Akiba elaborates this position by relating it to the political events of the day – the revolt against Rome led by Bar Kokhba whom Akiba suggested was the Messiah.[22] Rabbi Akiba taught that a generation could be saved by the virtue of its righteous people alone. It was because of the merit of the pious women of the day, said Akiba, that the Israelites were redeemed from Egypt. This interpretation helped Akiba adopt a positive attitude toward Bar Kokhba, for the people of that day were largely penitent and observant Jews. Thus Akiba saw Bar Kokhba's Messianic leadership as having been made possible by the virtue of the people of the day and as leading to a redemption of the nation and the land through the processes of world history. From the victory he hoped for from Bar Kokhba, Rabbi Akiba expected the fulfillment of Zechariah's prophecy, "There shall yet old men and old women sit in the broad places of Jerusalem, every man with his staff in his hand for every age."[23] Other Sages of the day, however, strongly disagreed with Akiba's identification of Bar Kokhba as the Messiah.

Following the failure of Bar Kokhba's revolt and the religious persecutions and dispersal of the Jews that followed, the thinking of the Sages focused on the challenges of finding redemption while living in the far flung diaspora communities. The failure of Akiba's view that redemption for Israel would come through the processes of history gives way to utopian-apocalyptic speculation such as the Apocalypse of Baruch or the idea of a "septennium" at the end of which the Messiah will come. The notion of redemption through the events of history is discarded in favour of redemption via supernatural events arising from the ruins of history. Toward the end of the second century C.E. a kind of "competition" develops between the Sages residing in Babylon with those still in the land of Israel over depictions of the disintegration of the world and the coming of the Messiah. Rabbi Johanan, the leading Sage in the land of Israel said, "If you see a generation continually declining, wait for him [the Messiah]" and "The son of David will come only in a generation that is wholly wicked."[24] This is a complete reversal of Akiba's earlier interpretation that it was the virtue of a generation that would usher in the Messiah. In Rabbi Johanan's vision the degree of degeneration prior to the Messiah's coming will be matched by the brilliance and glory of the days of the Messianic era.[25] Other Sages engaged in attempts to calculate exactly when the End would come – a tendency that has continued right up to the present. According to Urbach, however, when one takes into account all the apocalyptic stories and fatalistic views of redemption, there is still in the end a return to the dictum of Rabbi Eliezer that "If they do not repent, they will not be redeemed."[26] Or, in the view attributed to Rabbi Joshua b. Levi, the place of the Messiah – whether in the clouds of Heaven or as a poor man on earth riding an ass – is dependent upon the merits and deeds of the people of Israel.[27] Saunders summarizes as follows, "God provided salvation for all faithful members of Israel – all who maintain their place in the covenant by obedience and by employing the means of atonement provided by the covenant, especially repentance for transgressions."[28]

Medieval philosophy

In medieval Jewish philosophy two lines of thinking about redemption are found – the traditional supernaturalism and philosophical naturalism (in which there is strong influence from Greek thought). The traditional supernatural approach follows the thinking of the earlier Talmud. *The Book of Beliefs and Opinions* by Saadiah Gaon may be taken as an example of this approach, and describes the human condition and redemption as follows.[29] God creates the world out of goodness, with humans as its ultimate purpose. Humans, although created finite by God, are intended to be able to achieve redemption from their finite condition and achieve immortality. Thus God revealed the divine commandments through Moses at Sinai so that by following them humans could attain redemption. Two stages in the process of redemption are envisaged, both of which arise miraculously – the Messianic Age and the world to come. "In the Messianic Age the Jewish people will be restored to the Land of Israel and the first of the two resurrections will occur, that of the righteous Jews. When the Messianic Age ends, the world to come will emerge, then all of the dead will be resurrected and final judgement rendered. All who ever lived will now be infinite in time, the righteous enjoying eternal reward and the wicked eternal punishment."[30] Redemption thus includes not only the Jews as God's chosen people but ultimately all humankind.

The second approach of philosophic naturalism is exemplified by Maimonides in his *Guide of the Perplexed*.[31] In this line of thinking there is strong influence from Aristotelian and Neoplatonic concepts. In Maimonides' view the creation of the universe comes from God as a series of emanations during which humans and their world are created out of matter. Everything created from matter is good but finite in nature. Thus humans are finite and to achieve redemption must overcome their finite material natures. This is accomplished through metaphysical and scientific studies which give one an acquired intellect. "The acquired intellect enables man to gain ascendancy over his material desires during the life of his body, and at the time of death gives him immortality, since the acquired intellect exists separate from the body and is unaffected by its states or finity."[32] Unlike Christian medieval philosophy, there is no idea of original sin in medieval Jewish thought. "The Christian notion that mankind requires redemption owing to the guilt of original sin, which is incurred by every person as a consequence of Adam's disobedience in Eden, is completely foreign to the medieval Jewish thinkers."[33] In the Jewish view Adam is an example of religious righteousness whose spiritual excellence was ultimately inherited by God's chosen people, the Jews.

The Kabbalah

The Kabbalah, the mystical tradition of Judaism, developed alongside Jewish philosophy during the medieval period. According to the *Encyclopaedia Judaica*, the Kabbalists make no additions to the historic aspect of thinking about redemption as developed by the Sages or rabbis. But they make an original contribution with the idea that there is an "inner aspect" or "mystery" in the course of redemption that is expressed symbolically. Their basic idea is that the unity of God's good creation (symbolized as the Divine *Sefirot*) has been broken apart by human sin represented by the exile. The exile represents a state of creation in which human iniquity has caused a fissure in the mystery of the divine Godhead so that his name is not one – the *Sefirot* are no longer joined in divine unity. "The return of the people of Israel to its land at the time of redemption symbolizes the inner process of the return of the 'Congregation of Israel' or the *Shekhinah* (the 'Matron') to a continuous attachment to her husband."[34] The symbolism used represents the exile as a temporary separation between a king and queen – between God and his *Shekhinah*. Redemption is expressed as the restoration of their union as the united Godhead. Other Kabbalistic writers also employ the symbols of the garden of Eden from the book of Genesis. The "Tree of the Knowledge of Good and Evil" was originally one but was separated into two by the sin of Adam, who disobeyed God bringing sin and separation from God into being. These two trees symbolize (as did the earlier image of the king and his queen) exile as the experience of separation from God. Thus, during exile there are separate spheres of good and evil, holiness and impurity. At the time of redemption, however, God's essence, which is implicit in everything, will manifest itself causing a deep change in the structure of all creation so that the sense of separation will be overcome. In this metaphysical conception, "It is not only the oppression of Israel by the nations of the world which distinguishes exile and redemption, but also a deep and even utopian change in the structure of creation."[35]

Probably the most important further development of Kabbalistic thought was provided by Isaac Luria (1534–72). Central to Luria's thinking is that prior to creation, God, the Infinite (*en Sof*), engaged in an act of self-limitation to make room for the universe. Into the dark vacuum thus created, God projected divine light and "vessels" to receive the light. But some of the vessels were unable to sustain the inrush of light from the Divine (*en Sof*) and broke apart. The breaking of the vessels caused a deterioration in the worlds above and chaos in the world below. Instead of being uniformly diffused, the divine light was broken into sparks illuminating only certain parts of the world while others remained in darkness. Thus did light and darkness, good and evil, begin to compete with each other for dominance in the world. As Epstein puts it, "The Divine harmony was disrupted and the *Shechinah* exiled. At the same time, scattered hither and thither, the sparks of Divine Light intersected everywhere the darkness, with the result that evil and good become so mixed that there is no evil that does not contain an element of good, nor is there a good entirely free from evil."[36] The "breaking of the vessels" resulted in a state for all of creation of something like a "general exile," a disruption of the state of harmony God intended for the universe. Redemption, for Luria, is the restoration of a state in which the breaking of the vessels is completely mended and the harmony originally intended realized. The history of the people of Israel, with the history of all creation, is seen as a part of the process through which this universal harmony will be restored.[37]

Luria also refers back to Adam. All souls, he suggests, were created with Adam, although not all of the same quality. Some were superior to others, but all were good and in complete harmony. But when Adam sinned they all became tainted in varying degrees, resulting in a rupture of their harmony into a state of confusion among them. "The superior souls intermingled with the inferior, good with evil, so that the best soul received some admixture of the evil infesting the inferior souls, and the worst an admixture of good from the superior."[38] Thus although there is everywhere some impulse toward evil, this will come to an end with the coming of the Messiah sent by God to restore the original harmony to the souls of people and to all creation. But it is up to humans to take the lead in restoring this initial harmony, including the possibility of being reborn on earth to help others who are weaker to get rid of their evil.[39] Luria also suggests that the dispersion of the Jews into diaspora communities around the world has, for its purpose, helped the souls of other peoples to rid themselves of evil and realize redemption. The purified souls of the Israelites unify with the souls of other peoples to help liberate them from evil. When all the good has been separated from evil, both in individuals and in the whole of creation, then God's intended original harmony (*tikkum*) will be realized, and the world with all its peoples will be redeemed.[40] To initiate this process, Luria prescribed practices of asceticism, self-mortification, fastings and absolutions. These practices were not punishments for sin. Unlike those of Hindu *Yoga*, they were not seen as, in themselves, purifying the body, nor did they gain for one merit with God. They were simply seen as aids to one's spiritual discipline. Luria insisted that the body was as pure as the soul. "The body was a sacred vessel comprehending the Divine spark, the soul, and, as such, was holy and had to be kept in health and the utmost purity."[41] But Luria takes what today could be called an "ecosystem approach," for the redemption of the individual must be seen not as an end in itself but as playing a part in the greater goal of the redemption of the whole of creation.

These teachings of Luria had a great impact on Jewish mystical thought and on attempts to deal with the experience of good and evil. It offers a cogent explanation for the universal presence of good and evil in both the natural world and in our human condition. However, evil has no independent reality, rather it is the negative of good. It can be overcome by choosing good as individuals, by which we realize our inherent God-given good nature and aid in the universal process of redemption. Thus, what we do does matter in bringing forward the final redemption, and gives a sense of joy in what is done. Followers of this redemptive tradition in Judaism have expressed their joy in inspiring poetry and beautiful hymns. However, the *Encyclopaedia Judaica* notes that Luria's approach to redemption had one major problem. By emphasizing human initiative the way he did Luria left no real role for the coming of the Messiah or the grace of God in the redemption of the world. This problem was addressed and resolved by the later Hasidic movement, which solved the difficulty by distinguishing between "general redemption" (of the people of Israel) and "individual redemption" (the mystical redemption of the soul which has no messianic meaning). "This distinction is intended to limit human initiative to the realm of individual redemption and make general redemption once again dependent solely on the power of God."[42]

Modern Jewish thought

For modern Jewish thinkers redemption has been thought of in a variety of ways: as the ultimate triumph of good over evil, as the striving of individuals to reach self-fulfillment, as the achievement of social reforms, and as the reestablishment of a sovereign Jewish state. Hermann Cohen, for example, views the individual who commits sin as one who has departed from God's plan for the world and must be redeemed back to humanity so that God's ethical program for humankind can be actualized. For Cohen, then, redemption is the individual conquering his or her impulse to sin, for the good of the whole of creation – with God being understood as the redeemer who helps the individual to repent.[43] Thinkers who see redemption in terms of a triumph of good over evil include Martin Buber and A. J. Heschel. Buber, who also strongly influenced Christian thought in the twentieth century, thinks of redemption as the eradication of human-caused evil in history by sanctifying daily life – through seeing it as an encounter with God. Buber describes this encounter as a turning away from evil and toward God in our daily activities. God "enters into a direct relation with us men in creative, revealing and redeeming acts, and thus makes it possible for us to enter into a direct relation with him."[44] God helps make this possible by reaching out to us through grace – it is not primarily the result of our own seeking. "The *Thou* meets me through grace – it is not found by seeking. But my speaking of the primary word to it is an act of my being ... The *Thou* meets me. But I step into direct relation with it. Hence the relation means being chosen and choosing, suffering and action in one."[45] When this grace of God becomes manifest in our experience, redemption begins. Repentance helps to initiate redemption but should not be confused with it. Buber's understanding of redemption is strongly influenced by Hasadic teaching: "All that is necessary is to have a soul united within itself and indivisibly directed to its divine goal. The world in which you live affords you that association with God, which will redeem you and whatever divine aspect of the world you have been entrusted with."[46] Heschel's view of redemption is similar but perhaps places more emphasis on human action. The world needs redemption but this will not happen by God's grace alone. Humans have the task of preparing the way for redemption by separating good from evil. Heschel says, "All of history is a sphere where good is mixed with evil. The supreme task of man, his share in redeeming the work of creation, consists in an effort to separate good from evil and evil from good. Since evil can only exist parasitically on good, it will cease to exist when that separation will be accomplished. Redemption, therefore, is contingent upon the separation of good and evil."[47]

Another modern thinker, Franz Rosenzweig, sees redemption as the process by which humans and the world are united in a perfect harmony with God. Rosenzweig describes the relationships between man, God and the world under three headings: creation (God–world), revelation (God–man), and redemption (man–world). "The revelation of God to man implies God's love. Man's feeling of God's love 'redeems' man from his state of isolation and indeed from the supreme form of isolation – death, and its concomitant, fear. This love also awakens the response of love in man, and the binding together of man and God in love is the first step toward the redemption of the world, for the love spreads and is applied to other men."[48] After humanity is redeemed God's love unites humans with the world and thus redeems it too. Finally, God, as the unity of the whole, is also redeemed. As Rosenzweig puts it, "In this redemption God redeems the world by means of man and redeems man by means of the world. He also redeems Himself ... then true unity is created – God–Man–World. Eternity enters into being and death is pushed off and the living become immortals in eternal praise of redemption."[49] Another contemporary scholar, Mordecai Kaplan, uses the term salvation rather than redemption (which he argues has other-worldly connotations) and suggests that for modern people salvation must be seen in terms of this world. God is the inherent force in the universe that makes salvation possible, both for individuals and for society. For the individual, salvation means deliverance from the internal and external evils which prevent one from achieving a full and integrated personality. It is not a compensation for suffering but a result of human action which necessarily involves others and the world around us. Social salvation is "the pursuit of common ends in a manner which shall afford to each the maximum opportunity for creative self-expression."[50]

Modern Zionism, especially when conceptualized as a messianic movement, presents itself in terms of redemption. "Religious Zionist thinkers saw redemption as at least beginning in temporal terms with the return of Jews to Erez Israel and the building of the land."[51] According to A. I. Kook, "the hope for a return to the Holy Land gives modern Judaism its distinctiveness. It is the hope that sustains Judaism in its Diaspora communities in which return to the Holy Land is redemption." In Kook's thought, redemption has both a physical reality and provides a metaphysical hope for Jews everywhere. "Even nonreligious Zionist thinkers, while not necessarily using the term redemption, spoke in messianic terms or expressed themselves by concepts traditionally connected with redemption."[52] Redemption ideas such as the triumph of good over evil and the advance of social justice are part and parcel of the Zionist hope.

REDEMPTION, THE MESSIAH, THE RESURRECTION OF THE BODY AND THE AFTERLIFE

Judaism is unique among world religions in starting from the viewpoint that there is no survival after death – immortality is only through one's children.[53] Later the idea of a bodily resurrection becomes common, although rejected by one Jewish sect, the Sadducees. The notions of bodily resurrection, a Messiah and judgement in an afterlife, necessarily become engaged in discussions about redemption. It was during the period of the great prophets, immediately before the fall of Jerusalem and the exile of the Jews to Babylon that these ideas began to be introduced. Unlike others of their day, including the Greeks, Jewish thinkers thought of God and history not just in terms of Israel, but for all peoples and nations. Consequently redemption was envisioned for Israel and all of humankind – a world unity and harmony in which all people would reverence God as Lord of the earth. Given the chaos they witnessed around them in Judea, the prophets developed the idea that this ultimate unity of peoples under God would be ushered in by a "Day of the Lord" when God's judgements would fall on all the peoples of the earth, including Israel – a time of purifications and restoration of the world by God. Together with this thinking comes the idea of a Messiah who will introduce the rule of righteousness over all the earth, a time of universal redemption as well as redemption for Israel as a nation and for individuals (see the books of Isaiah, Jeremiah, and Ezekiel). This universal conversion to a new obedience to God's commandments would come by the Torah being engraved on people's hearts and in the consciousness of the nations. As a result the old order of personal selfishness and wars between nations would be replaced by a new order of justice, righteousness, and love. All of this is symbolized in the Messianic ideal, a suffering servant rather than a nationalistic king.

It was during the period of the Babylonian Exile and the Second Commonwealth (539 B.C.E. to 70 C.E.) that belief in an afterlife and bodily resurrection of the dead became widespread in Jewish thinking – perhaps as an import from Persian Zoroastrianism. From the second century B.C.E. on many texts suggest that the dead will be resurrected and raised to judgement. The book of Daniel is perhaps the best known. Written during the persecutions of the Jews by Antiochus IV Epiphanes (c. 165 B.C.E.), the text says "many of them that sleep in the dust shall awake, some to everlasting life and some to shame and everlasting contempt" (12:2–3). Segal comments that belief in an afterlife would satisfy a natural human craving for immortality and a scenario for a just and final retribution in times of persecution. But why a bodily rather than a spiritual resurrection? Perhaps, suggests Segal, it was to emphasize the inherent sanctity of the body as part of material creation – in opposition to Greek views which denigrated the body as weighing down the spiritual soul.[54] In the book of Daniel the bodily resurrection is placed before reward and punishment in the world to come. Resurrection to eternal life is the reward – especially for those martyrs who gave their lives for God and Israel. According to Urbach,[55] in the period preceding the destruction of the Second Temple by the Romans in 70 C.E., the rebellion against Rome is seen as the beginning of redemption, which would be ushered in by the appearance of the Messiah, the redeemer. As well as redemption for the notion of Israel, the Messianic redemption was thought of as a saving of individuals from their afflictions. Segal notes the range of views present in the thinking of the day.[56] Ben Sirach (discussed in Section I above) held with the Sadducees that death was final and that nothing survived beyond it. By contrast, the philosopher Philo, writing from the Jewish diaspora in Alexandria, argued for the immortality of the soul and mind, but not the physical body. Jesus of Nazareth maintains the Pharisaic belief in the resurrection of the body, with the early Christian Church believing that Jesus was the Messiah and that he himself experienced bodily resurrection.

Following the destruction of the second Temple and the loss of Jewish nationhood, only the Rabbis of the Pharisees seem to have survived. Their writings (in the Mishna and Palestinian and Babylonian Talmuds) show a consensus. The dead will be restored to their own bodies, not immediately after death but in the redeemed "world to come" that would be ushered in by the Messiah. In answer to the question as to what happens to people between their death and future resurrection, says Segal, the idea arose that disembodied spirits would live as individuals in a supernatural place.[57] Some Rabbinic texts suggest that the souls of the righteous awaiting resurrection would repose in the paradise of the "garden of Eden" while the souls of sinners would be consigned to "Gehenna" – the name of a ravine south of Jerusalem, notorious for having been the scene of a cult involved in child sacrifice by fire, which metaphorically came to denote a place of fiery torment reserved for the wicked after death.[58] These beliefs provided effective motivations for people to follow the commandments and avoid sinful behaviour. Segal observes that the belief in resurrection of the body had implications regarding the care of corpses. "Because the physical remains will one day be restored to life, they may not be destroyed. Therefore burial is the only sanctioned way of disposing of a corpse, and to arrange a proper burial was esteemed as a pious manifestation of the honour due to the dead."[59]

During the medieval period these same patterns of thinking about redemption, death, and the afterlife received further consolidation but with new lines of interpretation arising. For example, in the tenth century Rabbi Saadia Ga'on, under the influence of Greek rationalist philosophy, argued for a metaphorical understanding of "Gehenna" and the "garden of Eden" as spiritual states. He also suggested that "the initial resurrection in the Messianic era will include only Israel, whereas the righteous of all nations will be revived in the World to Come."[60] Yet another interpretation was offered by the mystical thought of the Kabbalists, who suggested that there were three different components of the human soul. The lowest, the animal soul (*nefesh*) is the part that is subjected to punishment in the grave. The spirit (*ruah*) is the part that is finally admitted to the "earthly garden of Eden." The immaculate soul (*neshamah*) originating in the divine *sefirot*, "and in the universal soul of the primordial Adam, ultimately returns to its divine source in the 'celestial garden of Eden.' In the more radical version of the theory, the *neshamah* was perceived as a part of God that is being restored to its source."[61] The Kabbalah thinkers also emphasize the need to bury the body at death. Cremation is flatly rejected. A key Kabbalah text, the Zohar, says that "there is a creation bone in the body which never suffers decay and, at the resurrection, the body is reconstituted from this bone."[62] If this bone is burned in cremation, resurrection is made difficult for God.

In modern Jewish thought, Orthodox Judaism has continued to understand redemption in terms of physical resurrection and afterlife as formulated either through the rationalistic emphases of Greek philosophy or the mystical speculation of the Kabbalists. Among non-Orthodox contemporary Jews, however, ideas about an afterlife are virtually absent, with most thinking of redemption and eternity being almost entirely as a religious dimension of this life.

3

Christianity

Christianity offers perhaps the clearest model of a salvation religion. Christian faith had its beginning (*c.* 30 C.E.) when Jesus came into Galilee preaching about God and saying, "Repent, and believe in the good news" (Mk. 1:14). In outline, Christian thinking runs as follows. The incarnation and sacrificial death of Jesus Christ formed the climax of God's plan for the salvation of humankind. This plan became necessary after Adam, the forefather of the human race, fell from grace into sin and death. God's plan to save humans from Adam's fate will be completed at the time of the Last Judgement when the second coming of Christ will mark the catastrophic end of the world. Because Jesus Christ is a Jew by birth and Christianity is born in a Jewish context, there are many echoes of Jewish ideas of redemption in Christian thought – along with some key differences. The notion of a Messiah, a saviour as envisioned by the Hebrew prophets like Isaiah, is taken over by Christians. Jesus Christ is identified as the Messiah. The idea of the bodily resurrection of the dead in also absorbed with the resurrection of Jesus from the tomb, as the first example. Unlike some Jewish ideas, however, the raising of all people from their graves for final judgement does not take place with the arrival of Jesus, the Messiah, but awaits his second coming following his death and resurrection. As was the case in Judaism, the saving activity of God is seen ultimately to engage the whole world, including both people and nature, and is thus thought of as the salvation history of the cosmos. Consequently the Christian division of time into the two periods: before Christ (B.C.) and Anno Domini (A.D.) – i.e., the years of the Lord. Unlike Judaism, Christian thought develops the notion that Adam's disobedience to God in the garden of Eden is inherited by all humans (and nature) as original sin and death. But there is considerable agreement with later Jewish ideas of an afterlife in which death will be overcome and a day of judgement will occur with appropriate rewards or punishments in Heaven or Hell. As we saw in the previous chapter on Judaism, these ideas regarding salvation evolve from the New Testament thinking of the early followers of Jesus through the history of the Roman Catholic, Protestant, and Orthodox churches to the modern thought of theologians today. In this chapter, first we will examine the Christian understanding of the human condition in which we all find ourselves and from which we need to be saved. Second, we will present the New Testament view of Jesus Christ as Messiah and Saviour, followed by an examination of the development of Christian thinking regarding salvation through the centuries. Finally, we will briefly examine the role of the resurrection, the body, and the afterlife in Christian salvation thinking.

THE HUMAN CONDITION

For Christians Jesus is not just a teacher or example but someone "whose life and death are accorded a cosmic significance that holds the key to the cure of the deepest ills of the human condition."[1] Jesus began preaching to the Jewish people of Galilee saying that the Kingdom of God was at hand, so they should repent and believe the good news. His Jewish hearers were familiar with the idea of God's Kingdom or rule for it was something they longed for after decades of Roman domination. Previous prophets had suggested that such a transformation of their lives would be brought about by God one day. Jesus taught that this was about to happen and that people should prepare for citizenship in God's Kingdom by radically changing their way of life. As Penelhum notes, this proclamation of Jesus did not make him that different from the Jewish Pharisees of the day – it was Jesus' requirements for entry into the Kingdom that made him different. The Kingdom was not for those whom one would naturally expect to enter – not the rich but the poor, not the teachers but the ignorant, not the righteous but the tax-collectors and prostitutes whom the righteous have avoided. But this does not mean that the requirements of life in God's Kingdom are easy. If anything the ethics of the Kingdom are more rigorous than those of Jewish Law. "It is not good enough that you do not have sexual relations with your neighbour's wife; you must not even want to. It is not good enough that you do not murder; you must not even hate. The Kingdom is for the pure in heart."[2] Salvation requires nothing less than an inner transformation which will enable us to act out of love for others rather than out of concern for following rules – and regardless of whether others deserve this love. The command of Jesus that we are to forgive one another as God forgives us is an example of such loving action.

However, our human situation is such that if we act from love then we put ourselves at risk. The only reason for doing this, says Jesus, is because it is the way God treats us. God loves us without regard to our merits and that is why we are to treat others the same way even if it leads to our being cheated, passed by on the promotion ladder, or even injured or killed. This seemingly utopian ethic of the Kingdom is not as imprudent as it seems at first sight, "If you really believe that you are a child of God, then you will be completely confident that God will see to it that your needs will be satisfied, and you will then not be anxious. If you do not believe this, love toward your neighbour is indeed foolish and hazardous. But if you do believe it (if you trust God), then you will be able to put your anxieties aside and act from love."[3] Thus to be ready for God's Kingdom when it comes you have to think, feel, and act now as if it is already here. And then, among those who do, there will be a foretaste of God's Kingdom already here. Salvation, in the form of the community of those living this way, as the nucleus of God's Kingdom on earth, will, through God's grace, grow like the mustard seed. Such was the analysis of the human condition and the prescription for salvation as presented in the early teaching of Jesus and recorded in the Gospels. His ethical teachings are intimately connected with salvation expectations. Jesus' hearers are told that God is in control of their lives, is poised to transform their world, and that they must turn toward God and act without reservation in the ways he demands. As Penelhum observes, "So the demands of the present are expressed in ways that make the sense they do because of his expectations of the future. If you do not share those expectations, the demands are hopelessly idealistic and psychologically impossible to satisfy."[4] Thus, there is a crucial connection between Jesus' ethics and his view of salvation and the afterlife.

After Jesus the most important influence on the Christian understanding of the human condition came from Paul, a Pharisee who began by persecuting the Christian community but was dramatically converted to it and became its most famous missionary and first theologian. Paul was a preacher to the Gentiles or non-Jewish communities of the Mediterranean world immediately after the death of Jesus (c. 33 C.E.). He expanded Christianity from a Jewish sect to a religion that was universal in its approach. In Paul's eyes the death of Jesus was a sacrifice that made possible the salvation of all people. And although the influence of Greek thought was very strong in

Paul's Gentile world, he still saw the human condition through the eyes of Hebrew scripture – but with some significant difference to the Jewish view we encountered in the previous chapter. In Paul's perspective each of us is in a state of sin because our original ancestors, Adam and Eve, disobeyed God. And somehow we have all inherited their rebellious nature and sinfulness, which for them and for us leads to moral corruption and physical death. Although we are all able to recognize that we are sinful and may well want to reform ourselves by turning back to God, alone we do not have the inner power to make this change. The role of Christ (the Greek word for Messiah) is to save us by reconciling us with God and giving to us this power. Unlike ours, Jesus' death was not a consequence of his sin; it was completely undeserved. In raising him from the dead, says Paul, God has proclaimed that those who repent and accept Christ will be forgiven. They will still die, but will do so with the assurance that, just as Christ was raised from the dead, they will be also.

Paul's message of salvation to his Gentile communities conveyed a sense of hope that contrasted with the gloomy conditions of their world – so gloomy that nothing less than the direct intervention of God in sending his son could turn things around. There were enemy astral forces (1 Cor. 15:24), and cosmic rulers so powerful that they had even crucified Christ the Lord (1 Cor. 2:8). All around were the inescapable forces of sin, decay, and death. Even the Jewish community, which God had chosen and to which God had given the Torah with its promise of redemption, had been compromised by sin (Rom. 7 and 8:2–3). As a Jew and a Pharisee, Paul taught that God was the creator of the world who had made all things "good" (Rom. 1:20; Gen. 1:3–31). What then had gone wrong? As suggested above, in Paul's view it was the sin of Adam that corrupted both human beings and the world of nature in which they live: "sin came into the world through one man and death through sin ... As one man's trespass led to condemnation for all men ... By one man's disobedience many were made sinners" (Rom. 5:12, 18, 19). Nowhere does Paul explain why nature is so dragged down by human sin or why God allows all of this to happen. Instead he concentrates on the way Christ has and will in the future put things right.[5]

The contemporary theologian Karl Rahner describes the human condition as feeling oneself to be incomplete, ambiguous, and full of suffering – both individually and collectively. We participate in sinful social structures before we become aware of their sinful character. Thus sin is social as well as individually chosen. As humans we try to become fit for salvation, but we receive it as a gift of God's love, not as a result of our capabilities. But humans are also in need of deliverance from their guilt. This guilt arises both from the state of original sin into which we are born and from the actions of our individual freedom, which always fall short of the expectations of God's Kingdom. As humans cannot remove their own guilt by undoing the consequences of their freely chosen actions, they depend on the love of God for forgiveness and redemption. Only as humans feel this freely given and unmerited love from God are they able to love God and other humans in return. Only on the basis of God's forgiveness of human sin is salvation from the trials of suffering conceivable. While suffering and death are the manifestations of guilt, complete forgiveness of sin can only come as the eschatological gift of God – it cannot be achieved by humans themselves. But humans may not always fully recognize their guilt. Guidance is needed to initiate humans into the recognition of their guilty situation. Here the teachings of Jesus play a major role in convincing each of us that we have fallen short and have not "gone the second mile." Only when our sinful guilt is thus recognized do we see our need for redemption and open ourselves to believe in the love of God "and accept it as unmerited and unconditional (and so therefore not ended by guilt), in the knowledge that even to accept this love is the work of this love."[6] Yet all of this occurs within the context of human freedom in which the will of God manifests itself as an offer to forgive and save us. Thus we are free to accept or reject the forgiveness and salvation God offers through Christ. Let us see how this is presented in the New Testament.

THE NEW TESTAMENT VIEW OF JESUS AS SAVIOUR

The New Testament Gospels (interpretative biographies written from the perspective of the preaching of Jesus as saviour) use the words saviour (*soter*) and salvation (*soterion*) sparingly. As Oxtoby observes, "The angels announce to the shepherds in Luke 2:11 that a saviour has been born in Bethlehem, but otherwise it is chiefly in John's theological account that the Messiah is saviour (Jn. 4:42) and that the world through him is saved (Jn. 3:17)."[7] Yet in the Gospels Jesus' saving work is more broadly conceived than in the New Testament letters. Jesus not only dies for human sins, but the miracle stories of his healing ministry are seen as evidence of his saving power. In many of the healing miracles, restoration to health is viewed as a sign of salvation. Jesus cures physical and mental diseases and restores people to a right relationship with God. His healings, miracles, exorcisms, and works of mercy are all manifestations of the wholeness that is a part of the salvation God provides. But Jesus' teaching and acts also make clear that salvation also involves the removal of the barrier of sin, which separates humans from a sense of living communion with God. In the Gospels, especially the Gospel of John, Jesus' death upon the cross is seen as a sacrifice by which this barrier was forever removed and a new way opened to God for repentant humans. Even during his lifetime Jesus' ministry is marked by the authoritative way in which he brings salvation to people by forgiving their sins. Unlike some views where the emphasis is placed on a future "day of the Lord" or a time of

Jewish political supremacy, Jesus' salvation takes effect in the moment in which sin was actually ruining the human life of the individual. The salvation Jesus offers is not to take effect at some future date in the midst of apocalyptic scenes, but right now in the direct experience of God's forgiveness. "God in His love, man in his need, Jesus speaking for God and bringing God near – these are the abiding three in Christian salvation; and their relationship to one another is never more vividly presented than in the stories of forgiven sinners told in the Gospels."[8] Yet for Jesus, as for the Hebrew prophets, this present personal experience of God's forgiveness is not the end but only the foretaste of the future when God's divine movement will be complete and his Kingdom on earth fully come. Although fixed on the future goal, Jesus also emphasizes salvation as a present experience in which one's ethical action is needed to prepare the way for the full realization of God's Kingdom on earth. Peter Toon summarizes the view of the early Christians: "He went to the cross as the Suffering Servant, the Lamb of God, and the obedient Son, in order to make salvation (in its fullest and everlasting sense) a permanent possibility and gift from God to mankind. What the Old Testament sacrifices had imperfectly achieved, he, as the pure lamb of God, perfectly accomplished. He was gloriously vindicated in his resurrection from the dead and exaltation into heaven."[9] Thus his disciples preach that salvation comes in no other name than the name of Jesus. Jesus had taught them to pray. He brought God to them in the immediate forgiveness of their sins. Jesus won from them trust in himself as Saviour. In their language and Jewish background, only one word seemed to fit him – Messiah (Mt. 16:16).

In the Book of Acts and the New Testament letters the physical healings and benefits that come from salvation are not emphasized as much as being in the right relationship with God through Jesus Christ in the power of the Holy Spirit. This "right relationship with God via the forgiveness of sins" is a salvation experience that is seen to be based on what Jesus has done – he is the Lord and Messiah (Christ) seated at God the Father's right hand in heaven. Paul, following Jewish rabbinic teaching says that this salvation also refers to a future event when God will judge the world, destroy the wicked, and establish his Kingdom on earth. In his letter to the Christian congregation in Rome Paul says, "For salvation is nearer to us now than when we first became believers; the night is far gone, the day is near" (Rom. 13:11–12). For Paul, Jesus is the saviour who is to bring about this transformation: "we await a Saviour, the Lord Jesus Christ, who will change our lowly body to be like his glorious body, by the power which enables him to subject all things to himself" (Phil. 3:20–21). For Judaism, salvation meant not only obeying the rules of the Torah but also surrendering to the will of God. For Paul, belief in Jesus is emphasized as a basic requirement. Jesus is understood not just as a rabbinic teacher but as the "Lord" sent by God to save us from our own sinful natures and from oppressive cosmic powers. As Paul puts it in his letter to the congregation in Rome, "If you confess with your lips that Jesus is Lord and believe in your heart that God raised him from the dead, you will be saved" (Rom. 10:9). Belief is required but also trust in the form of a personal commitment (see Gal. 2:19–21). In Paul's view belief and trust in Christ give rise within the believer to the experience of God as loving father – as taught by Jesus in the Gospels. For Paul, the death of Christ for sinners was proof of God's love (Rom. 5:8) and the basis for the Christian confidence in God's love (Rom. 8:38–39). This is different from Judaism in that for Paul Jesus is not only the teacher of faith but the one who makes it possible for us sinners.[10]

As noted above Paul held that God was the creator of the world who had made all things good, however, the disobedience of Adam, which we and the cosmos in general inherit, resulted in our sinfulness. But Paul does not explain why God allowed things to happen this way. Rather he focuses on the ways Christ has and will put things right. In some passages, Paul suggests that Christ undoes the harm of Adam by behaving in opposite ways: Adam was disobedient, Christ was obedient; Adam brought death, Christ brought life. Using the language of the Temple sacrificial ritual, Paul suggests that, through his complete obedience to God, "Christ served as a form of blood sacrifice, expiating sin through his blood (Rom. 3:25), thereby making humans 'righteous' or 'justified'. Through his coming in the flesh ... and his dying in the flesh, Christ has begun a transformation of the cosmos and humanity."[11] Thus Paul, using a childbirth image, talks of the whole of creation and those who have committed themselves to Christ as "groaning in travail" towards a new birth in which we, our bodies, and all of nature will be saved or redeemed (Rom. 8:22–23). And, says Paul, it is this faith that gives us hope. Those who believe experience the first fruits of salvation through an infusion of Christ's Spirit via baptism (joining with Christ's cosmic body, the Church), or by taking part in the communion meal of eating his body and drinking his blood (1 Cor. 11:23–27) – the reality of which is variously understood depending on one's Church denomination. Becoming "in Christ" in these ways leads to a moral and social transformation of life in which one is to sin no more. But baptism only begins this transformation from being sinners – as Paul's letters of exhortations, threats, and scoldings show when members of the early Christian churches fail to live morally as they should. However, their righteous conduct, together with their faith and baptism in Christ gives them confidence that they will be saved from the impending wrath of God. According to Paul, "Those saved in Christ, in the brief period before his return defeats evil ... can only 'groan' as they await their 'adoption as sons' – and, most specifically, the redemption of their bodies (Rom. 8:23)."[12] This transformation of the believer's body, says Paul, will be like the resurrection of Jesus' body – the flesh of one's earthly body will change into a "spiritual" body (1 Cor. 15:44). Let us now examine how later generations of Christians, claiming to follow Paul's teachings, interpret God's creation (Genesis), the human condition and salvation as a gift through Christ.

SALVATION THROUGH THE CENTURIES

Later generations of Christians formed differing views on God, physical creation, Jesus, Paul, and salvation. There was increasing influence from the Greek context. An early response to Paul and the Christian message took a Gnostic form.

Gnosticism

In the Gnostic approach, a person was saved by a revelation of hidden knowledge (*gnosis*) as to who one was and what one's human condition really was. All Gnostics were dualists and polarized spirit/flesh, High (spiritual) God/Lower (Jewish, fleshly) God, etc. Only the spiritually perfect person (Paul's *teleioi*, 1 Cor. 2:6) could understand God's revelation – that one's true self, "a divine spark or higher spirit, was trapped in the cosmos of the lower god, stuck in flesh essentially alien to it. But those in Christ, as Paul had promised, could be free of the power of the flesh."[13] This theology demanded an ascetic ethic in regard to food and sex in an effort to free oneself from the body, while still in it, and in this way achieve salvation. Salvation, in the Gnostic view, was from ignorance more than from physical death. Once one's pure spiritual soul, with Christ's help, broke free from its entrapment in the fleshly body, it would then ascend to the higher spiritual Heaven and be united with him.

This Gnostic interpretation of salvation quickly gave rise to an opposing anti-dualist, anti-Gnostic branch of Christianity which won the struggle as to how to understand the teachings of Paul and established itself as the "orthodox" Christian position. A universal ethic of celibacy was rejected, as was the Gnostic interpretation that Jesus did not really live in the flesh. Earthly, material reality was not rejected and was bound more closely to ideas of God, Christ, and salvation. Leading thinkers in this line, such as Justin Martyr, Tertullian, and Irenaeus argued that if God is the source of earthly creation (as Genesis says) then creation, even if fallen, cannot be alien to God. Unlike the Gnostic dualists, who imagined salvation as the spiritual passage of an individual (with Christ's help) through an evil cosmos, these "orthodox Christian thinkers" saw salvation as involving Christ's transformation of the cosmos itself. For those who believed and were baptized "in Christ" the suffering, ignorance, and evil of the human condition was being transformed by Christ's Spirit, and would be fully overcome at Christ's second coming "when Creation itself would be healed of Adam's lingering damage and the flesh itself redeemed. Christ himself, therefore, had really had a body, and had shown in his own resurrection what the human flesh would become."[14] And at his second coming, those "in Christ" would rise in their bodies and experience a transformed and redeemed earth. Salvation involved the recovery of a just society (as in Judaism) along with a redemption of bodily existence and of nature itself.

The Christian Fathers

The battle between dualistic Gnostic interpretation of the Christian message and the "orthodox" scholars (who came to be called the "Church Fathers") continued for several centuries. The orthodox Christian thinkers also argued against other communities such as the Jews. Among the Church Fathers we will focus especially on Origen and Augustine.

Origen (185–254 C.E.) offers a systematic exposition of salvation. A teacher of Greek philosophy and the leading biblical commentator of the day, Origen held that humans were rational beings created by God with free will. In the time before the creation of the world these rational beings turned from God and fell varying distances – some to be angels, some descending into human bodies, and the most wicked becoming devils. The material world was created by God out of nothing as a means of discipline, with earthquakes and plagues as reminders to humans that earthly life is not their true home. The purpose of the created world is to place humans, with their varying levels of spiritual merit, in educational situations where they could come to choose, freely, to return to God and be redeemed from their fallen state. Salvation, then, is the grand educational purpose for which the cosmos was created and by which all souls – even those who have fallen the farthest – can be saved. Salvation, for Origen, is the restoration of all souls to their original blessedness, for none, not even Satan (the most fallen) has so lost rationality and freedom as to be beyond redemption.[15] Although God never coerces, he may punish people with the intention of helping them reform their ways. Although life in the fleshly body is not the spiritual home of the soul, it is not seen as a state of entrapment (in contrast to the view of dualistic Gnostic thinkers). Rather, for Origen, bodily life is not the cause of the soul's sin but is the opportunity given by God to the soul for salvation. As Fredricksen puts it, "Origen praises flesh as the medium of redemption, and a dazzling index of the ingenuity of a generous, loving Creator."[16] In Origen's scheme, one soul had not fallen but had remained in adoring union with God, the Father. Uniting with this soul, the divine Logos (Word), the second person of the trinity of Father, Son, and Spirit, became incarnate on earth in a body derived from the Virgin Mary. This is the climax in God's plan for the salvation of the world. Although Christ's soul, like other souls, had free will, the intensity of its union with the Logos (God's word) destroyed all inclination to turn from God. This spiritual intensity was manifested not only in Christ's soul but also in his body when Jesus was transfigured in the resurrection.

For Origen, Christ's resurrection is not an epoch-changing event in itself but rather provides a perfect example for people to follow in their educational struggle to use their free will and make the rational choice to give up sin and return to communion with God – the position from which each of us started before the fall. Salvation is an educational task by which the fallen rational soul is restored "from matter to spirit, from image to reality, a principle directly exemplified in both the sacraments and in the inspired biblical writings, in which the inward spirit is veiled under the letter of law, history, myth, and parable."[17] The role of the biblical teacher is to perceive within the material body of scripture its soul or spirit and to show forth its existential meaning for the individual Christian in his or her educational struggle for salvation. God's help or grace is given by the revelation of scripture and the "school for souls" is provided by the Church with its teaching and sacraments. In this life we receive elementary education and in the life to come higher education – including a period of punishment in Hell if that is what it takes to bring us to our senses. But in the end no one will be lost, everyone will be saved. Because of God's respect for human freedom, for some salvation may take time, including even an education that continues in the afterlife. But God's love will ultimately triumph and Christ's educational task remains unfinished until all souls have returned to God by their own free choice. In the redeemed state, we will retain our bodies (as Christ did) but they will have nothing to do with earthly life (our secondary educational state of existence). For Origen, the soul's body, which distinguishes it from other souls and from God (who has no body) is literally metaphysical – a transformed or transfigured body. In this context the defeat of death is the overcoming of ignorance by means of understanding offered through scripture, which leads us to choose to return to God our Father by following the example of Jesus.

Augustine was influenced by Origen but put forth his own view of salvation in his masterpiece, the *City of God* (413–26

C.E.). The book was written a hundred years after Emperor Constantine converted to Christianity and made Christianity the dominant religion of the Roman Empire. But it was composed only a decade or so after Alaric entered Rome (410 C.E.) and pillaged the city for three days.[18] Hearing of these events from his home in North Africa, Augustine saw this attack on the Empire by barbarians from without and within as defining "a new division between church and state and a conflict between 'matter' and 'spirit' resulting from the fall of man and original sin."[19] In a unique way Augustine combined Greek and Hebrew thought. Strongly influenced by Paul's letters, Augustine regarded salvation as a cosmic process designed to gather an elect group "to fill the places of the fallen angels and so 'preserve and perhaps augment the number of the heavenly inhabitants.'"[20] The role of society and government is to keep order in a secular city (in an intrinsically evil world), which contrasts with the heavenly City of God. The Christian Church had the role of sanctioning government and protecting civilization from the excesses of sinfulness that threatened chaos and disorder.

How did Augustine see all of this cosmic drama playing out in individual human lives? When God created humans in the garden of Eden, God created them with fleshly bodies, male and female, joined with souls. Therefore, said Augustine, the Genesis account of creation clearly implies that God chose to make humans with gendered fleshly bodies as the natural habitat of the soul even before the fall. This means that God had always intended humans to be fruitful and multiply by the sexual union of male and female. But sex before the fall would have been different. Then, said Augustine, without the urgings of lust, "every member of the body was equally submissive to the mind and, surely, a man and his wife could play their active ... roles in the drama of conception without the lecherous promptings of lust, with perfect serenity of soul and with no sense of disintegration between body and soul."[21] What changed this paradisaical experience of sex was that humans, although created by God with the freedom to choose not to sin, disobeyed God's command. In punishment, God struck humans in the offending part of their nature, the will itself. And since mind or soul are seen by Augustine to be intimately connected, this punishment of the will also manifested itself in the body – "There appeared in their body a certain indecent novelty which made nakedness shameful, and made them self-conscious and embarrassed."[22] As Fredriksen puts it, "Whereas prior to the Fall the capacity for physical pleasure would have been coordinate with the will, therefore, it escaped conscious control."[23] This disjuncture of body and soul, created by human disobedience, has resulted in the soul – which God created as a loving partner for the body – being separated, unwillingly, from the body at death. "From Adam on, then, humanity has found itself in a penal condition of ignorance and mortality, through the morbid condition of lust."[24] Thus, as Paul puts it, the will not only is unable to control the body, it can no longer even control itself: "The evil I do not want to do, I do" (Rom. 7:19). The soul, with its divided will, was naturally created to love God, but since the fall has turned in upon itself in self-love. Human nature, body and soul, is now turned away from God and toward ignorance and death.

How then does God save us from this fate? In Augustine's view, God justly condemned the human race, but he has mercifully chosen some individuals for salvation. As we are all sinners, it is not a question of God saving the just or the righteous. It is by God's grace alone that any sinners are saved. Paul himself is seen by Augustine as the key example. Although a murderer and persecutor of the Church, God inexplicably saved him. But, like Paul, even those who receive God's grace will still struggle with sin and die. How then will God save us? Augustine finds his answer by reading Paul's letter to the Romans. Humans will be regenerated through the revelation of God in the flesh – the incarnation and resurrection of Christ.

Those whom God has chosen in the Church, through baptism experience their first regeneration. Their final regeneration, however, will be when God raises all humans in a resurrection of body and soul, for final judgement to reign with his saints in his eternal Kingdom.[25] It is in this last act that God will finally resolve the human condition. And this last resurrection, notes Fredricksen, "*must* be with a body made of flesh: only reunited with the flesh can the soul be truly complete."[26] When Paul states "flesh and blood cannot inherit the Kingdom of God" (1 Cor. 15:50), one must remember, says Augustine, that by "flesh" he meant the moral orientation of one's will, not one's physical body. With one's resurrection, at the time of Jesus' second coming, the fleshly body will be raised spiritual, "meaning that with the wound in the will closed and the soul healed, the body of flesh will again, without effort, follow the dictates of the spirit in all things: man will no longer be capable of sinning."[27] Thus, for Augustine, to be saved is to be raised with one's body of flesh to dwell with God in the heavenly city. While nature is not saved, humans are.

Thomas *Aquinas* (*c.* 1225–74) has come to represent the Roman Catholic approach to salvation. For Aquinas, in his *Summa Theologiae*, being saved requires that one assents inwardly and outwardly to the articles of faith of the Catholic Church out of love for God and out of a trust in him. Thus, salvation involves two themes: faith as intellectual assent; and faith as formed by love. By assent Aquinas means that faith is an inward act of believing, and believing is to think with assent to the propositions proposed for belief by the Church. Faith is different from scientific knowledge for in the case of knowledge one has evidence or logical inferences that establish truth. The truths of faith are not self-evident and require assent to them by a deliberate choice of the will. So for Thomas, to know scientifically "is to see that something is so, either by immediate sense-perception or by logical inference, and faith is the conviction of things not seen (Heb. 11:1)."[28] This does not mean that faith must be uncertain, for if you are unsure about what the Church proposes for your belief you do not have faith but only opinion. On the cognitive scale, faith falls midway between scientific knowledge and mere opinion. "All three are modes of assent to truths proposed, whereas *doubt* is withholding assent because you cannot make up your mind ... Faith differs from opinion because it is certain; and it differs from knowledge (in the strict sense) because its certainty is not derived from self-evident truth."[29] Why should one trust the propositions proposed to us for belief by the Catholic Church? Because they rest on the authority of God who revealed them in the Bible, and they have been summarized in the creeds set forth by the Church which cannot err. For Thomas then, saving faith is equated with submission to the infallible authority of the Church in terms of trusting what is to be believed. To have faith thus means to give your assent to the articles of faith as presented by the Church's creeds and to be ready to accept anything else that may be proposed for your belief by the Church. A heretic, for Thomas, is one who disbelieves even a single article of faith. If one neglects to follow the teaching of the Church out of ignorance or honest error then one may be excused. But if one knowingly and stubbornly disbelieves the Church's authoritative teaching then, like an infection in the body, such a person must be cut off from the Church and from salvation.

But intellectual assent is not the whole of the approach to salvation adopted by Aquinas, there is the second part – namely that faith is formed by love. Love or friendship for God is what forms the habit of faith which makes the mind assent to things unseen. Assenting is the inward act of faith while confession is its corresponding outward act. And the love that forms the habit of faith is not something we acquire for ourselves, rather, it is a habit infused by God. As Gerrish puts it, for Aquinas "only love can 'form' faith: it enlivens the act of faith, making it spring from a lively communion with God."[30] For Thomas saving faith requires not just bare assent to the propositions of the Church, but an act inspired by love for God.

The Reformers

Martin *Luther* (1483–1546 C.E.) came to think of salvation primarily in terms of grace – a free and forgiving gift from God shown to us in Jesus Christ, so that our conscience, "forgiven and cleansed, may be at peace, and that the soul, free from the burden of guilt, may serve God with a joyful, spontaneous, creative obedience."[31] For Luther it is one's own direct personal experience of God's saving grace that is key. Luther was countering what he felt to be a one-sidedly intellectual concept of faith in the Roman Catholic Church following Aquinas. Luther did agree with Aquinas that intellectual assent was involved in faith, but he insisted that it was something more as well – namely one's own personal experience of God's grace and forgiveness that arises from trust in the promises of the gospel. Luther suggests that there are two ways of believing:

> One way is to believe *about* God, as I do when I believe that what is said about God is true ... This ... is knowledge or observation rather than faith. The other way is to believe *in* God, as I do when I not only believe that what is said about Him is true, but put my trust in Him, surrender myself to Him and make bold to deal with Him, believing without doubt that He will be to me and do to me just what is said of Him.[32]

The believer, for Luther, does not merely accept what is said about God in scripture or by the Church, but appropriates it for oneself in personal experience. Unbelief, therefore, is not heresy but lack of trust. Faith, says Luther, "is a luring, daring confidence in God's grace, so sure and certain that the believer would stake his life on it a thousand times."[33] Here we find the idea that the just person shall live by faith, and Luther's translation of Romans 3:28 as, "We hold that a man is justified by faith alone apart from works of law" to guard against perversions that might seem to make salvation dependent on human achievement or a reward for work done.

The difference between Aquinas and Luther (between Catholicism and Protestantism) is not so much an absolute contrast as a reversal of priorities. As Gerrish puts it, "Thomas speaks mostly of assent to propositions about God, Luther of trust in God. But Thomas thinks of the propositions as the medium in which we have faith in the Godself; and Luther never for one moment suggests that we could trust God without believing anything about God."[34] For both, saving faith requires that one commit oneself to God. A difference between them arises over the role of Jesus Christ in all of this. For Aquinas, Christ is the cause of the grace that infuses the love of God into one's soul and makes possible assent to the teachings of the Church. For Luther, it is Christ as made present in the gospel story and who engages one to trust in God as loving father that makes possible saving faith. For Luther, the crucial thing is the way we perceive of and experience God in Christ – not as a remorseless judge but as a loving, forgiving father. Rather than in the creeds and statements of the Church, Luther's knowledge content came from the scripture itself. As Gerrish summarizes, "In the gospel, Luther heard – and gave his trust to – the God who says: 'Whoever takes hold of this Son and of Me or of My promise in Him through faith – to him I am God, to him I am Father ...' And this 'sure knowledge of God,' as Luther called it, is precisely what Calvin, too, understood by faith."[35]

John *Calvin* (1509–64) almost summarizes Luther's analysis of faith but adds the emphasis that Protestant faith involves "recognition." Calvin's writing on faith is found in book 3, chapter 2 of his *Institutes of The Christian Religion.*[36] He sets forth the nature of saving faith as it is found in the Word of God, especially as presented by Paul. But in addition to his appeal to scripture, Calvin takes into account actual Christian experiences. For example, while Calvin admits that faith ought to be certain, he allows that we cannot imagine any certainty that is not tinged with doubt. Calvin defines faith as follows: "Now we can agree on the right definition of faith if we say that it is firm and certain knowledge of the divine goodwill toward us, based on the truth of the free promise in Christ, and both revealed to our minds and sealed on our hearts through the Holy Spirit."[37] As Gerrish summarizes, Calvin's definition of faith has four parts. "Faith is (1) knowledge (2) of God's goodwill ... faith, in the sense defined in (1) and (2) rests on the truth of the free promise in Christ and (4) is revealed to the mind and sealed on the heart by the Spirit."[38] This kind of knowledge is not focused on propositions about God, or Church creeds. It is closer to what we would call knowledge by personal acquaintance or direct experience rather than knowledge by description. Calvin uses the term "recognition" to characterize this kind of faith knowledge, which is a response to the disclosure in Jesus Christ of God's goodwill for us. Like Luther, Calvin sees faith as the recognition of the goodwill of God disclosed in the gospel and linked with the image of a loving Father. As Calvin states:

> Faith does not rest on ignorance but on knowledge – knowledge not simply of God, but of God's will. We attain salvation not because we are ready to embrace as truth whatever the church has prescribed ... but rather when we *recognize that God is a father who is well disposed to us* (now reconciliation has been brought about through Christ) and that Christ has been given to us as our righteousness, sanctification and life. It is by this knowledge, I say, not by surrendering our minds, that we obtain access to the kingdom of God.[39]

For Calvin, saving faith involves the heart as well as the brain, and proves itself in the suffering and obedience one goes through amidst the challenges of life. It is because of God's fatherly goodwill towards us that our faith can remain constant in the ups and downs of life. For Calvin, unbelief is the opposite of faith – thinking that God is against you. In Christ one sees

God as God really is – loving Father rather than enemy, even when God disciplines one and expects obedience, just as loving parents do.

Protestantism

Protestantism followed the lead of Luther and Calvin and taught justification by grace through faith alone, the priesthood of all believers and the power of the Holy Spirit. The Protestant doctrine of justification by grace through faith emphasized the biblical picture of a loving and gracious God. This view countered the Reformers' interpretation of the Roman Catholic Church in which the flow of God's grace came through the Church's sacramental system and its hierarchy, and where the believers made sacrifices designed to appease and please God. "They would attend mass, bring offerings, show sorrow, do penance – which might involve self-punishment or compensatory good works – until God would be gracious. The leaders of the church, from priests through bishops and popes, mediated the transactions."[40] The Protestant Reformers believed that this approach could be used by the Church to keep rules under Church control and people in uncertainty or terror. It was this vision of Catholicism that led Protestants to their conception of salvation by justification through faith alone as seen in Paul. Paul was constantly striving to please God by following the Law as set forth in the Old Testament. Yet he failed and was filled with doubts about his salvation. Paul's conversion in the New Testament involved a turning away from his struggle to be worthy under the Law to a free acceptance of God's grace in Christ. Following Paul's example, saving faith meant that a person so identified with Jesus Christ that when God looked at him or her, God did not see the sinner but rather the merit that Christ had won through his self-sacrifice on the cross. By seeing his Son rather than the sinner, God could justify and save one, even though the person was still a sinner.

Moving from Paul's teachings in the letter to the Romans, the Reformers taught that for their own times the work of the Holy Spirit was crucial. For the sinner living all these years after the time of Christ's life and death, it was the presence of the Holy Spirit now that made Christ's action contemporaneous with the sinner's quest. Through preaching the sinner learned of Jesus Christ's sacrifice and death, and of the power of the Holy Spirit to save. Through Christ the believer stood before God in a new light. It was not that grace was infused into the soul until an individual became acceptable to God, but rather that, while still a sinner, God accepted and saved. "Christ's death on the cross was then the only 'transaction' that mattered between God and man. The sacraments [baptism and communion] reinforced the relation and brought new grace, but no pretense was made that the human subject had achieved satisfaction before God or produced enough merit to inspire God to act."[41] While Catholics worried as to whether they had provided enough merits or achieved enough good works, the Protestant vision had the believers standing before God completely justified and freed from these nagging worries. However this did not mean that the believer did not have to do good works. In the Reformers' view, while good works did not *win* salvation, they were integral to its working out.

Protestant teaching also broke down the medieval role of the clergy and Church as the mediator between the believer and God. In the Protestant "priesthood of all believers" perspective, the biblical teaching maintains that all believers can relate directly to God and have a share in spreading the good news of God's forgiveness in Christ. Christians were to take responsibility for each other's salvation. Any Christian could present the needs of all others to God by caring and praying for one another. Thus, for Protestants, there was an equality of status between clergy and laity and a common calling that all Christians are to be agents of God's word and grace – a shared "calling" in which clergy were not more meritorious than laity, and monastic vocations virtually disappeared. The idea of "the priesthood of all believers" meant that no single Church could monopolize the mediation of God's grace since there were believers in all Churches; Roman Catholic, Lutheran, Calvinist, Anglican, and other Protestant denominations. Authority shifted from the teaching of the Roman Catholic Church, for example, to the authority of the Bible, which each person could read and interpret for oneself. While Protestant Churches had the role of maintaining order and discipline, the Reformers saw final authority to reside in the Word of God that many simply equated with the Bible. As opposed to the medieval emphasis on scholastic theology (e.g. Augustine and Aquinas) or on the Church's sacraments for salvation, Protestants rediscovered the Bible and its teachings as the primary impetus for saving faith.

While Protestant philosophers of the seventeenth and eighteenth centuries were strongly influenced by rationalism and the success of science, by the mid-eighteenth century John Wesley gave birth to the evangelical or Methodist movement in England. Wesley gathered a group of students of the Bible together at Oxford and initiated a missionary preaching expedition to Georgia in North America. He emphasized the necessity of conversion if one was to be saved, and devoted his life to evangelistic preaching in England. Adopting a legal constitution in 1784, Methodism spread rapidly in industrial areas, in the hilly countryside and in the American colonies. The Methodist approach to salvation emphasized the aspects of feeling and conscience that Protestant orthodoxy tended to neglect. It gave a devotional impetus to the doctrines of grace and justification, especially as expressed in the Christian hymns of writers such as Charles Wesley (1707–88). In the American colonies the Congregational or Baptist approach was popular. Public testimony to one's experience of a saving conversion was required in a religion of the heart that stressed the immediate experience of salvation. This powerful movement came to be called "The Great Awakening" and was led by Jonathan

Edwards (1703–58), an intellectual mystic and powerful preacher in New England. His preaching conversions began in 1735 and for the rest of the eighteenth century waves of revivals spread throughout the colonies. Evangelical preaching and conversion of the Methodist, Congregational, and Anabaptists types permanently influenced the Protestant approach to salvation right up to the present. In evangelical "testimony meetings," one tells the story of God's dealings with one's soul and receives the Church community's acceptance and the community's confirmation of one's self-understanding.

The need for a personal commitment was also emphasized by the Protestant philosopher/theologian Friedrich Schleiermacher, who in his *Speeches on Religion* (1799), suggested that although one can define religion in general, one cannot be religious in general (the view of many people today). To be saved, says Schleiermacher, one must settle in a specific religion – you have to "pitch your camp" somewhere.[42] Karl Barth (1886–1968) pushes it further maintaining that as Christians one belongs somewhere in a Christian denomination.[43] This is what is meant by a "confessional faith" – one is Christian only as one commits oneself to God through Jesus Christ in a particular community of believers. Confessions of faith, says Gerrish, are reminders whose main task is not to uncover heresy, but, through constant recall and restatement, to preserve identity.[44] They maintain a common language and a unity of fellowship in the Church community. Confession in this sense is not just telling others of one's own saving experience with God, but also calling to mind the ancient Christian creeds that Protestants share with both the Roman Catholic and Orthodox Churches. For all Christians, the basic foundation and confession has always been: "Jesus is Lord (or Christ)." But a confessional faith is more than its creeds or confessions of faith; "it includes hymns and histories, the biographies of heroes and the treatises of theologians, reports and pronouncements of church assemblies, inherited forms of worship and polity, and – along with everything else – an intangible *ethos* that is easier to recognize than define."[45] Nor does the emphasis of the Reformers on the Bible reject the grace of God that the sacraments confer. As Calvin put it, "the sacraments confer grace by arousing faith, and grace is contained in them as Christ is contained in the gospel."[46] Calvin valued tradition, as did the Roman Catholic Church, but held that one's duty as a Protestant is to test tradition by God's Word in the Bible. A Roman Catholic scholar, George Tavard, observes that before the Protestant Reformers provoked the Catholic Church to a one-sided emphasis on tradition, the Catholic view had been that salvation requires both scripture and tradition – the Council of Trent, for example, "respects the classical view: Scripture contains all revealed doctrine, and the Church's faith, which includes apostolic traditions, interprets it."[47] At Vatican II, the Roman Catholic Church understood itself as the sacrament of salvation for the world. Of special significance for Catholics are the sacraments of baptism and, for those who have fallen away after baptism, the sacrament of penance. Although salvation is seen by Vatican II as coming only from the grace of God, humans are empowered to work with God, since grace sets in motion new morality. Vatican II also allows that there is grace outside the Church so that salvation is possible for innocent atheists and adherents of other religions who have not heard of Christ.[48]

Eastern Orthodoxy

The Eastern Orthodox Christian Churches have been separate from the Roman Catholic and Protestant Churches since 1054 C.E. They are mainly Greek and Russian in ethnic character. The Orthodox theology of salvation is expressed in the Easter hymns where Christ is the one who "tramples down death by death," and on Good Friday already wins the victory. Salvation is understood not in terms of Christ paying the debt for the sin of Adam – as in the medieval West – but in terms of "uniting the human and the divine with the divine overcoming human mortality and weakness and, finally, exalting man to divine life."[49] What Christ accomplished by his death and resurrection is to be taken on freely by all those who are "in Christ." Their goal is "deification" which means raising the human to the divine status prepared for humanity at the time of creation. Salvation involves "participation in the already deified humanity of Christ as the true goal of Christian life, and it is accomplished through the Holy Spirit."[50] Orthodox feasts such as Transfiguration or Ascension are popular because they celebrate humanity glorified in Christ.

SALVATION AND THE AFTERLIFE

Having traced the history of salvation in Christian thought, let us conclude this chapter by examining conceptions of death and the afterlife. Christian theology often proclaims that the Church is the interim Kingdom of God on earth, and looks forward to the day when God's Kingdom will be fulfilled. Paul and his successors thought of this fulfillment as involving resurrection from the dead, which is guaranteed for Christians by the resurrection of Christ (1 Cor. 15). Paul says, "As in Adam all men die, so in Christ all will be brought to life; but each in his own proper place: Christ the firstfruits, and afterwards, at his coming, those who belong to Christ. Then comes the end, when he delivers up the kingdom to God the Father, after abolishing every kind of domination, authority and power. For he is destined to reign until God has put all enemies under his feet; and the last enemy to be abolished is death" (vv. 22–27). According to Paul, Christ will return and then those who belong to him will be raised. In answer to the question as to what sort of body one might have when raised from the dead, Paul says that our earthly bodies will be succeeded by a spiritual body – like the body of a person who has been redeemed from the corruption we received from Adam. This incorruptible spiritual body, says Paul, will have glory and power and be immortal.

If this is Paul's view as to the resurrection of the body, what about the question as to who will be raised at the time of the second coming of Jesus? While some Christians have believed that Christ will save everyone, the dominant position is that everyone has had a chance to accept or reject the path of salvation. Those who accept are described as "in Christ" and will be made alive at the end time. The question then arises: are those who are not saved to be raised or not? Various answers have been suggested in Christian history. Do they die and disappear or are they raised only to be condemned? The dominant idea seems to be that those who are not saved will be separated from the saved when all are raised at the Last Judgement. They then go to opposite destinations imagined in the first century as a three-storey universe with Heaven above for the saved and Hell underneath the earth for the not saved. The activity of Jesus was also thought of in this three-storey way: God sent him down from Heaven to earth where he lived for a time, was crucified and descended into Hell and then rose from the dead and ascended into Heaven. From Heaven he will come down to earth again at the end of time.

The early Christian community also thought that Christ's return would take place soon. But as the years passed, expectation of Christ's second coming diminished with various speculations arising as to what would happen between one's physical death and one's resurrection when Christ returned at the end of time to sit in judgement. No clear answer was reached. What was certain, however, was that if one had not accepted Jesus Christ as Lord and been saved during one's lifetime, there was no opportunity to do so after death. This raised the question of the fate of those who lived and died before the coming of Christ. It is answered by the First Letter of Peter that says Christ "made his proclamation to the imprisoned spirits" (1 Pet. 3:19), which is interpreted to mean that between his death and resurrection Christ descended and preached to those who had lived before his birth, so that they too would have a chance at salvation. A further interpretation offered by the Roman Catholic Church, is the idea that for those who heard the good news about Jesus and could have responded, their fate at death may be tempered by purgatory. The idea of purgatory is for those who at death are already deemed to be saved but who are guilty of sins for which they have not done adequate penance before death. By going through a period of purgation or redemptive suffering it is thought they could complete their penance and be ready for Heaven. The idea of purgatory was accepted by Catholics and the Eastern Orthodox, but rejected by Protestant Christians.

Contemporary Christians struggle with how to adapt the biblical and early Christian views of death and the afterlife to the modern world. Modern science has made it impossible to hang on to ideas of Heaven and Hell located in a three-storey universe. So, some Christians today tend to think of Heaven and Hell as descriptions of the way we live our lives here and now – as the Kingdom of God on earth. On this view salvation amounts to the transformation of one's personality in this life. Others think that it is essential for Christians to believe that there is an afterlife. In their understanding, the improvements required in the "saved" personality will never be completed in this life. As Penelhum puts it, "If this promise of continuing change were not to be realized – if there were no hereafter – all the Christian language about salvation, eternal life, cleansing, and the rest would be utopian and false. But if it is true, then the afterlife is a necessity, not just a doctrinal bonus."[51] But there is much debate today over how to interpret Paul's biblical ideas about death, resurrection, and Jesus' second coming. While some Catholic, Orthodox, and evangelical Christians cling to a literal first century C.E. understanding of the texts, many today are searching out ways to adapt Christian belief to modern thought. Modern evolutionary science and its survival of the fittest process tells us that death is a natural part of life – that death is not an aberration introduced into nature by human disobedience, but rather a key part of life's creative selection process. Thus one might not accept the teaching of Paul that human death came into the world via Adam, or the idea that death itself should be viewed as a curse. One can also debate how Jesus' resurrection should be understood: is there really a physical body involved or not? While scholars like Paul Gooch[52] argue against a body, others such as Oscar Cullman[53] maintain that the *soma pneumatikon*, or resurrection body, of Jesus is physically real. Resurrection, says Cullman, implies not only "the Holy Spirit's taking possession of the *inner* man, but also the resurrection of the *body*."[54] This resurrection body is a new creation of matter which is unique in Christ and which Christians can also look forward to in their future resurrection at the end time, if one follows Cullman's physical interpretation.

Christian feminist theologians have also turned their attention to the question of how to understand salvation in relation to death and afterlife. Focusing salvation on the physical resurrection of ourselves from earth to Heaven, say the feminist scholars, has devastating practical consequences for humans and nature. This otherworldly goal of salvation implies that the earth does not matter as much as Heaven and that this life matters little when compared to the next. Consequently Christians, as individuals or in powerful government and corporate positions, have not treated the earth with respect. Sadly, the implications of the traditional understanding of salvation, with its afterlife focus, do not bring one to challenge such sins, for ultimately they do not seem to matter. Similarly, women, children, and the poor have been exploited without adequate protest when the community's focus has been too fixed on the heavenly afterlife as the place where all will be put right. Seen in this way salvation has sometimes spawned apathy rather than justice and at times even encouraged unhealthy martyrdom. Christian feminists today are seeking to redefine salvation and the afterlife so as to remove the devastating practical consequence inherent in traditional approaches. One scholar, Sallie McFague, suggests that salvation must be brought down to earth.[55] In her view it is then immediately apparent that the health and well-being of earth, air, water, plants, animals, and humans must be a very significant part of what salvation is about. "Humans must acknowledge that the responsibility for the salvation of creation is ours, not God's. We are called, at this point in history, literally to choose between life and death. We can choose to participate in the ongoing salvation of creation, or we can choose to participate in its destruction."[56] Salvation, in this feminist perspective, is clearly not a once-and-for-all event, nor does it have a lot to do with resurrection – unless by that is meant the resurrection and restoration of the earth and a just human society. As to the question about what happens to us after death, the feminist reply is that we just don't know. What we do know is that energy is neither created nor destroyed, that everything that makes up the universe can be converted from matter into energy, and that ultimately we are made of the same stuff as the stars. "Perhaps the only way to ensure our eternal salvation is to teach our children and their children to respect and honour all of creation, from the least to the most awesome aspects of the cosmos."[57]

4

Islam

Islam has several terms with salvation-like qualities that together paint a multicolored notion. A key term used for salvation is *"najat"* which means escape or deliverance from the fires of hell to the pleasures of paradise. *Najat* is not a common term in the Qur'an, the scripture of Islam, appearing only at 40:41, "I call you to salvation, and you call me to the Fire."[1] Although the word *najat* (salvation) is used only once in the Qur'an, the basic aim of Islam is salvation in the sense of escaping future punishment. Muhammad saw himself as the last in a line of prophets (including Abraham, Moses, and Jesus) that Allah or God had sent to warn his people of impending doom. The clear sense of Muhammad's teaching in the Qur'an is that obedience and submission to Allah is the way to salvation, for Allah is merciful. Unlike the previous chapter where we saw that for Christianity salvation is redemption from sin, here in Islam salvation is conceived in terms of escape from the fires of Hell by following God's guidance (*huda*). The Qur'an is *huda* in that for those who obey, it brings them out of darkness and into light, out of polytheism and into worship of the one God, out of lawlessness and into loving obedience which, at the Day of Judgement, will land one in Heaven rather than Hell. This Qur'anic guidance leads to *falah* (success, prosperity) in this world and the next. *Falah*, as salvation, depends on human effort as well as God's mercy in following the Qur'an's teachings. As Fazlur Rahman puts it, for Islam there is only success *(falah)* or failure in the task of building an ethical and social order in the world by submitting oneself to the Qur'an. Salvation can be achieved in this world as well as the next but it all depends on submission and obedience.[2] M. A. Quasem makes the dependence of salvation on *huda* or guidance from Islam quite clear: "Scripture is guidance for mankind and what this guidance aims at is his salvation, whether in this world or the world to come. This salvation is the central theme of . . . the Qur'an."[3] With this overview of the Islamic approach to salvation, let us begin our more detailed study by examining the Islamic understanding of the human condition in which we all find ourselves.

THE HUMAN CONDITION

Nowhere does the Qur'an teach that human nature is basically flawed and must be regenerated. In this Islam is quite different from the Christian concept of original sin according to which all humans are inherently tarnished by Adam's disobedience to God in the garden of Eden and thus need regeneration to be saved. Although the Qur'an acknowledges that Adam did indeed sin, his sin was not passed down to all humankind. Like Adam individual humans have the capacity to sin, but it is not predetermined. The view of human nature presented in the Qur'an has a more positive tone. Humans are not cast out of the garden of Eden as a punishment for their sinfulness, but rather are exiled so that they can use their free will to choose to work with God in creating a moral and beautiful world. As Nomanul Haq puts it, God created Adam to work on earth as a kind of viceregent *(khalifa)* – someone to work with God at the historical level of earthly existence. "The human exit from the

Garden, then, was ... akin to natural birth – a baby coming out of a mother's womb, a bird breaking out of an egg, or a bud sprouting forth from a branch. Indeed, like nature, Adam had to evolve, morally, spiritually, intellectually – just as a baby grows into adulthood, and a seed grows into a lofty tree."[4] Thus the human condition in Islam does not involve the recovery from a fall so as to regain some original state of glory, but rather entails the fulfilling of a set of obligations given by God in the Qur'an.

The basic idea is that in creating the universe, God has brought into being both nature and humans under obligations to be observed. Nature, unlike humankind, has no faculty of will and no possibility to choose. Therefore, nature carries no moral onus and merits neither reward nor punishment. Nature spontaneously and naturally fulfills its God-given obligation (*amr*) by observing the law of nature which God created. Humans, by contrast, are endowed by God with the ability to choose and are thus morally liable for decisions they make in living life. Like nature humans are created by God for the purpose of bringing about, through God's guidance, a moral order here on earth. Unlike nature, however, the fundamental nature of humans is that they are created with the freedom to choose but also with the obligation (*amr*) to observe the Law of God, revealed in the Qur'an, and in so doing to help bring about moral order in human history. In this way humans can merit salvation. Simply put, by doing good and rejecting evil through fulfilling God's obligations as set forth in the Qur'an, humans evolve morally and spiritually, reaching ever-new glories. By providing for both good and evil in the world, God has placed humans in a state of moral tension. But this offers a creative opportunity, "for in order to avoid the ever-present evil, humanity had to keep harking back to, and supplicating for the succor of God – and this struggle kept in tact a transcendental moral anchorage in human life."[5] According to Islam, it is in this struggle that the moral, spiritual, and intellectual potential of human nature is realized. In this context evil, like good, is part of the larger struggle that, in the end, is seen to be serving God's purpose. Nor is nature left out, for by naturally fulfilling God's obligation, without the possibility of violating it, nature works with and encourages humans to make good choices and thus together to actualize God's ecological plan for creation. Indeed Islam sometimes speaks of two books of guidance, the "book of nature" and God's word in the Qur'an, as together setting forth Allah's *amr* or obligation to be followed if salvation is to be realized in this life and the next.

The impact of this new diagnosis and prescription for the human condition on the first Muslims in Mecca is seen in the following appraisal by Ja'far to Negus (king of the Christian Abyssinians) regarding the impact of Muhammad and the teachings of the Qur'an on the transformation of their lives:

> O King! We were an unenlightened people. We used to worship idols, eat carrion, commit abominable acts, sever the bonds of kinship, treat our neighbours meanly, and the powerful amongst us used to devour the weak. We remained in this state until God sent us a messenger, one of us. We knew his lineage, truthfulness, faithfulness, and purity. He called us to God, to profess belief in His oneness and to serve Him; to repudiate the idols and stones that we and our ancestors used to worship. He adjured us to truthfulness in speech, delivering the trust, maintaining the bonds of kinship, being good neighbours, to abstain from committing unlawful acts or shedding blood; he forbade us the commission of acts of indecency, uttering false testimony, devouring the property of the orphan, or slandering chaste women; he ordained for us prayer, giving alms, and fasting ... Thus we trusted him, accepted him and followed him.[6]

For his followers, Muhammad was a prophet and a messenger of God. God's message, that continued to be revealed to Muhammad until his death in 632 C.E., was the Qur'an. Let us now examine in detail the teachings of the Qur'an on salvation.

SALVATION IN THE QUR'AN

Islam has been called a "natural religion" in which humans are seen as created with a sound nature (no idea of "original sin" here) and given a clear choice to obtain salvation.[7] The various aspects of salvation are presented in the Qur'an in several key terms which we will now review. A foremost quality needed for salvation is to be a "believer."

Amana (to believe)

Belief in God (Allah) is held by the Qur'an to be required for salvation. Salvation is described as a reward for those who believe in God's messengers (4:151). God will extend mercy and guide in a straight path to himself all who believe in him (4:174). Believers, in the Qur'an, include Jews and Christians since Moses and Jesus are recognized as valid messengers or prophets. Those who believe in God and act uprightly "will have their reward with God and experience neither fear nor grief" (2:59) at the Day of Judgement. Robson notes that according to 19:61 "God, who always fulfils his promise, will admit those who repent, believe, and act uprightly to the Gardens of Eden. Qur'an 25:70–76 says God will substitute good deeds for the evil deeds of those who repent, believe and act uprightly."[8] Believing alone however, is not enough; moral behaviour is also required. Believers are also described as never giving false witness, passing by vain things with dignity, and praying that they may be god-fearing models to their spouses and children. As a reward for their belief and good behaviour, they will be welcomed to Paradise with greetings and salutations of peace. In that garden with rivers they will be rewarded by being allowed to remain there forever.[9]

Foremost among believers, and indeed those who have set the example for the rest of us to follow, are God's messengers or prophets. God rescues Moses from the evil designs of Egypt's

Pharaoh, and Moses leads the people of Israel to freedom (44:24–31). Noah is named as a prophet whom God saves from unbelievers and from storms at sea.[10] Prophets such as these are named in the Qur'an as examples of how God saves believers and their families. About the deliverance of Abraham and Lot the Qur'an says,

> And We made them chiefs who guide by Our command, and We inspired in them the doing of good deeds and the right establishment of worship and the giving of alms and they were worshippers of Us (alone). (21:73)[11]

It is in these discussions of the prophets of the Bible that the Qur'an makes clear that prophets such as Moses and Jesus and their true followers have received God's deliverance. According to the Qur'an (23:88) God's deliverance and forgiveness awaits all who heed the prophets.[12] Since warners or prophets have been sent to all peoples, so the offer of God's mercy, enlightenment and salvation is extended to all people. Acceptance of God's mercy depends upon the promptings of divine grace.[13] A major theme running through the Qur'an's retelling of the stories of biblical prophets such as Abraham, Noah, and Moses is that their belief in God occurs in the context of being surrounded by sinful disbelievers. Thus the example of the prophets teaches that God saves one from sinful surroundings that would land one in the fires of Hell to the joys of Paradise if one believes and lives a righteous life.[14]

Najat *(deliverance, salvation)*

Although *najat*, the actual word for salvation, occurs only once in the Qur'an, its forms, derived from the same root, occur often "expressing deliverance from [worldly] calamities and occasionally in connection with eternal salvation."[15] As Denny notes, a typical usage is in the Qur'anic presentation of the biblical Jonah story:

And Dhul Nun [i.e. Jonah] – when he went forth enraged and thought that We would have no power over him, then he called out in the darkness, "There is no god but Thou. Glory be to Thee! I have done evil."

So We answered him, and delivered him out of grief [*najjaynahu min al-ghamm*]; even so do We deliver [*nunji*] the believers [21:87–88].[16]

Like Jonah, believers will be delivered not only from physical and moral calamities in this life (7:64) but also at the Day of Judgement and resurrection from the fires of Hell. Belief in God and striving with one's goods and person in God's way will result in "forgiveness of sins and fine dwellings in the Garden of Eden."[17]

The Qur'anic idea of *najat*, salvation, is not so much deliverance from the power of sin as from eternal punishment. As Qur'an 3:14 puts it, "O our Lord, we believed, so forgive us our sins and protect us from the punishment of the Fire."[18] The important thing about this deliverance (*najat*) is that it is rescue from the fires of Hell to the better circumstances of Heaven. The escape is from the punishment of sin, not from the bondage of sin as in Christianity – thus it does not involve a change of one's human nature but rather the reward of enjoying the pleasures of Paradise. So Qur'an 39:62 states, "*Allah* shall rescue (*naja*) those who fear him into their place of safety" and Qur'an 3:182, "Whoso shall escape the Fire and be brought into Paradise shall be happy."[19] Salvation is contrasted with Hell and described in terms of escape from Hell to the pleasures of Heaven.

Denny emphasizes, however, that *najat* or salvation should be understood in the Qur'an at a deeper and more subtle level than just surface rewards or punishments. In the Jonah passage (21:87–88) God delivers the prophet from *al-ghamm* variously translated as "worry," "grief," affliction," "distress," and "anguish."[20] "The point appears to be that God delivers His servants in this life from the darker depths of the human condition – from fear, dread, anxiety, and other forms of emotional suffering."[21] Rather than saving one from some external threat, deliverance, in this context, is the releasing of a person from the evil one generates from within. Denny observes, "Jonah had to call out in the darkness to God, glorifying Him while confessing his own sin, before God would deliver him from *al-ghamm*. This is not to suggest that man can in any way save himself; rather it is to acknowledge that, without human recognition of God's lordship, salvation is impossible."[22] Consequently, deliverance is only for believers. But fortunately God offers mercy and guidance to all.

Rahma *(providential mercy)*

Through providential mercy (*rahma*) God has willed forgiveness for wayward humankind. This mercy is unconditional and central to God's nature yet it is balanced by God's justice. While God's mercy is offered to all, his love (*wudd*) is given only to virtuous believers. As 19:96 puts it, "Surely those who do believe and do deeds of righteousness – unto them the All-merciful shall assign love (*wuddan*)."[23] God does not love the unbelievers (3:32). However, God's mercy and forgiveness are freely extended to all, unbelievers as well as believers. But "God does not suspend His justice in the granting of mercy and forgiveness; rather, these can be seen as expressions of it, assuring mankind of God's noble purposes, however veiled they may be to human eyes."[24] It is for a just purpose that God has created the heavens and the earth. As Fazlur Rahman points out, the beauty and harmony of creation are critical clues to God's nature. "Indeed, there could have been just empty nothingness instead of this plenitude of being ... *but for the primordial act of God's mercy.*"[25] The existence of creation itself, including we humans, is seen by Islam as a part of God's mercy that sets the stage for our choice to believe and obey God, and thus merit salvation. The truth of God's saving mercy and forgiveness are conveyed to us through both the beauty and sustenance of nature and the words of the Qur'an. Both, therefore, can serve to guide us to salvation as the concept of *hudan* makes clear.

Hudan (guidance from God)

God's mercy and initiative for the salvation of humans from meaninglessness, straying, and error is expressed as guidance or *hudan*. Guidance is given in God's signs (*ayat*) which come to us through two main forms, the world of nature and historical events such as the appearance of the prophets. Thus these signs offer to humans two kinds of revelation or guidance (those God built into nature and the teachings of the prophets) which everyone can understand if they would simply pay attention. In Qur'an 30:20–25 God's signs include:

> that He created you, of yourselves, spouses, that you might repose in them, and He has set between you love and mercy. Surely in that are signs for a people who consider. And of his signs is the creation of the heavens and the earth, and the variety of your tongues and hues. Surely in that are signs for all living beings ... for a people who hear.[26]

According to the Qur'an God created people with an inbuilt capacity to receive guidance leading to deliverance if they will but attend to God's signs. Some, however, ignore this naturally given guidance through perversity or laziness. For those who "see" guidance is present in the signs of nature all around us, and is also built into our own human natures. So, as Qur'an 30:30 teaches, all that is required is that we are obedient to the innate nature that is within – for then one would be living the pure faith or religion within – unfortunately though, most people don't know it. Thus the need for the prophets and their books, which help people to "see" the original true religion (*din al-fitra*) that is already within. Of these the greatest guidance is given by Muhammad and the Qur'an. The Qur'an enables humans to see and understand the guidance God has inbuilt in creation. So the Qur'an is called *bayyina* or "that which makes things clear" (98:1) and also *rahma*, a "mercy" (17:82). As Denny summarizes, "It is in the Qur'an that the guidance which is behind God's plan of salvation for straying people becomes specific and applicable, both as a reminder of the long history of man's losses and triumphs (mostly the former) before Muhammad's time and more immediately as promise and warning for those to whom the Qur'an has been sent down."[27]

The Qur'anic concept of *hudan*, notes Robson, suggests that salvation is not just a matter of human effort that will bring the reward of Paradise in the afterlife, but is a process under the guidance of God who freely offers help to all who will accept. Humans are not left to themselves. As the Qur'an says, "God will guide the heart of everyone who believes in him" (64:11), so that "those who believe and do what is right will praise God for guiding them to Paradise. They recognize their guidance as coming from God, whose messengers brought the truth" (7:40f).[28] There seems to be a special form of guidance given after death to warriors killed in God's service: "God will guide them and reform their condition, and cause them to enter the garden" (47:5–7).[29] In Qur'an 6:90 Muhammad is exhorted to follow the guidance given to the prophets who preceded him. Robson summarizes,

> Abraham was guided (16:122; 26:77f.) ... Some prophets were given books. God wrote for Moses our tablets for the guidance of the people (7:142). God gave Jesus the Injil [Gospel], containing guidance and light (5:50). The Torah and Injil were sent down in earlier times as a guidance for the people (3:2).[30]

The ultimate guidance is the Qur'an given by God through Muhammad. But revealed words alone are not enough. They must be accepted and acted upon as in the case of upright believers. Then God's mercy and justice offer a foretaste of salvation in this life through *furqan* (the Muslim community), which can provide deliverance from immediate peril (8:29). More often, however, *furqan* signifies deliverance through the separation engendered by the Qur'an from the unbelievers, staying on the straight path, and the formation of a distinct Muslim community.[31] Another term important for God's guidance or *hudan* is *sakina*. Perhaps a borrowing from Judaism where the Hebrew term "*skechina*" indicates the presence of God in the world, the Qur'anic *sakina* refers to a sign of divine help God would send down on believers. "For example," says Denny, "in 9:26, it is a kind of assurance sent by God to Muhammad and the believers at the battle of Hunain ... In 48:4 we read, 'It is He who sent down the *sakina* into the hearts of believers, that they might add faith to their faith ... and that He may admit the believers, men and women alike, into gardens underneath which rivers flow, therein to dwell forever, and acquit them of their evil deeds.'"[32]

Falah *(success, prosperity)*

With reference to salvation, *falah* refers to the balance Islam seeks to obtain between this world and the next. Speaking of those who will avoid Hell, Qur'an 87:14 says, "But he will prosper, Who purifies himself." The translator notes that *falah* here refers to "prospering" in the highest sense of attaining bliss.[33] Fazlur Rahman makes clear that *falah* as salvation depends on human effort as well as the divine action of God. This is illustrated in Qur'an 3:64, "O People of the Book! [namely Jews, Christians, and Muslims] Come [let us join] on a platform [literally: a formula] that may be common between us – that we serve naught except God." The human effort required is that the believers in all these religions cooperate "in building a certain kind of ethico-social world order and is not in the nature of contemporary forms of 'ecumenism,' where every 'religious' community is expected to be nice to others and extend its typical brand of 'salvation' to others as much as it can! For Islam there is no particular 'salvation' there is only 'success' [*falah*] or failure [*khusran*] in the task of building the type of world order we are describing."[34] Muslims, as well as believers from the other religions, can work towards salvation in this world and the next, but, as Qur'an 62:10 says, first there must be submission and obedience. Denny observes that *falah* requires a great effort, which is the inner meaning of *jihad* (9:88). For those who succeed in such a struggle, they will receive eternal life in the gardens of Eden and dwell forever in God's good pleasure.[35] Salvation thus is very much an idea of success and prosperity. The means to achieve this success have been discussed in the notions of mercy and guidance described above.

An important point is that central to this notion of salvation as success is the Muslim community itself, the *Umma*. Salvation is "intimately linked with the Islamic way of life, in which there is (ideally) no distinction made between religious and secular realms ... The *Umma* is indispensable to salvation, for it is the nurturing environment for living the Muslim life."[36] The behaviour of those within the community who will realize prosperity as the inheritance of an eternal abode in Paradise includes: humility in prayer, avoidance of vain talk, payment of *zakat* (an alms payment based on property exceeding a certain minimum), maintenance of sexual morality, honoring one's pledges, and careful observance of prayers.[37] In all of this, as noted earlier, salvation is equally open to women and men. This is made explicit in Qur'an 33:35 which says that God has prepared forgiveness and a fine reward for Muslim men and women. Qur'an 57:12 "speaks of the day when male and female believers will be ... welcomed to their abiding place in the Gardens through which rivers flow."[38]

Having surveyed the key terms relating to salvation or deliverance in the Qur'an, let us now examine the Muslim understanding of the means to salvation and note some of the differences of interpretation that obtain between the major divisions within Islam: Sunni, Shi'a, and Sufi.

THE MEANS TO SALVATION

We have seen that in the Qur'an the root idea of salvation is escape from Hell's torment to the reward of Heaven's delight. But exactly how one escapes has been a matter of some debate in the development of Islam's theological thinking. As Miller points out the problem has its roots in the Qur'an. Muhammad was not a philosopher or systematic theologian and so there are a variety of views in the Qur'an as to how one achieves salvation. These variations, and at times contradictions, have been used over the years to support a variety of positions. Miller suggests that these may be grouped under six headings for purposes of study.[39] He comments that a person may hold to one viewpoint or to a combination of these theories and still remain a good Muslim. We will look at each of these six approaches to salvation in turn.

Salvation by the will of Allah

Some Muslims suggest that human salvation is hidden in the mystery of God's activity – either God's predestining will or God's mercy. Those who maintain predestination emphasize that a person is damned or saved by the action of God's will. This is a common approach and harkens back to passages in the Qur'an such as Qur'an 7:177, "He whom God guideth, and they whom He misleadeth shall be the lost," or Qur'an 6:125, "And who God shall be pleased to guide, that man's breast will be open to Islam; but whom he shall please to mislead, straight and narrow will he make his breast."[40] These passages and many others show a major trend in the Qur'an to see salvation and damnation solely in the will of Allah. Orthodox (Sunni) Islam has picked up these passages in the Hadith (sayings and doings of Muhammad or his companions) and later theological commentaries. Umar is reported to have said,

> When Allah creates a servant for Paradise, He bids him perform the actions of the people of Paradise and thereby causes him to enter Paradise. And when Allah creates a slave for the Fire, he bids him perform the actions of the people of the Fire and thereby causes him to enter the Fire.[41]

Hadith reports such as this suggest strong support for the idea that God has predetermined who will go to Hell and who will end up in Paradise. However, Muhammad, in the Qur'an and the Hadith, at times emphasized God's total control, and at other times he presented humans as having free choice and responsibility for their actions. Consequently, the idea that God predestines who will go to Heaven or Hell has been constantly challenged, though it eventually won out as the position of orthodox or Sunni Islam. A group called the Mutazilites did challenge this view, maintaining that humans have free choice and responsibility for their actions. They dominated Islamic thinking for about one hundred years (850–950 C.E.) but were displaced by al-Ash'ari who lived in the tenth century.

Al-Ash'ari argued that in the final analysis it is God who acts and determines who ends up in Paradise or in Hell.[42] His reasoning runs as follows. Since God alone is the creator, all must ultimately be attributed to him. As he is the Lord he can do what he likes with his creation. God is above everything and at the same time is the cause of everything, including who ends up in Heaven or Hell. Regarding the problem of how then did it matter what humans did or did not do, al-Ash'ari developed a theory that humans "acquire" the acts which God creates. "God does not will absolutely. He wills something to be the act or acquisition of the human being. Man is connected with his acts in the sense that he gives them the character by which they merit recompense."[43] In this way al-Ash'ari tried to create some room for human responsibility and action within the choices God had already made. Al-Ash'ari's approach picked out those passages of the Qur'an that emphasized God's total control over creation and pushed that thinking to its logical conclusion – humans are little more than pawns in God's hands with no real free choice or responsibility for their actions. Al-Ash'ari tries to temper this result with his theory of the acquisition of God's action by humans. Because al-Ash'ari's theory had a strong basis in the Qur'an it was accepted and is reflected in the creeds of orthodox Islam. For example, the Creed of al-Nasafi (c. 1050 C.E.) states, "Allah is the Creator of all the actions of his creatures, whether of Unbelief or of Belief, of obedience or disobedience."[44] And al-Taftazani, a commentator on this creed, spells out the implications of this doctrine clearly: "So if the creature purposes a good action Allah creates the power to do good, and if he proposes an evil action, Allah creates the power to do evil, and he thus loses the power to do good."[45] Thus it would seem that it is God's choices and not those of humans that determine if they are to be delivered to Paradise or sent to burn in the fires of Hell.

Does this view, which seems to exaggerate the Qur'anic emphasis on God's all-powerful will, still represent the thinking of orthodox Islam today? Miller thinks that it does:

> It is probably correct to say that most orthodox mullahs, if questioned, would generally agree with the interpretations of al-Ash'ari and al-Nasafi, and in that agreement they would be holding true to a leading motif in the Qur'an. But not only that. This doctrine is the dark background that lies behind the thinking of many an ordinary Muslim as he considers salvation ... for many it is the reason why they are driven to say: "I cannot say, I am saved, I can only say, I am saved if God wills."[46]

But Miller also notes that many contemporary Muslim theologians sharply disagree with this approach. The famed Egyptian thinker Muhammad Abduh held that right and wrong are not created by God's will, for reason can distinguish good and evil without waiting for revelation; and that religion requires independence of mind and thought.[47] Another noted scholar, Fazlur Rahman declares, "To hold that the Qur'an believes in an absolute determinism of human behaviour, denying free choice on man's part, is not only to deny almost the entire content of the Qur'an, but also to undercut its very basis ... [the] invitation to man to come to the right path."[48] This issue is a problem, not only for Islam but for other religions, such as Christianity, that simultaneously hold that God is the all-powerful creator of the universe and that humans, as a part of that universe, have been created with real freedom of choice.

Salvation by the mercy of Allah

As we have seen the Qur'an frequently speaks of God's mercy and grace. Thus some Muslims have thought of salvation under the umbrella of God's mercy. God is thought of as being tender-hearted, more inclined to mercy than to wrath. As Qur'an 59:7 says, God has sent his revelations "that He may bring you forth from darkness into light; and lo! for you Allah is full of pity, merciful." Miller comments, "Moreover He is named Al-Ghaffar and Al-Ghafur, the Forgiver and the Very Forgiving One, who places veils over the sins of humanity, and the Qur'an mentions His forgiveness hundreds of times. Surely He will also forgive His people who have truly struggled to follow His path."[49] Some passages in the Qur'an are very explicit. It is the mercy of God which will lead people to Paradise (Qur'an 7:47) and save them from Hell (Qur'an 6:16). From one perspective God's mercy seems to function by awakening people to his guidance. At other times his mercy seems to sustain his people on the straight path. As God's followers are inspired to do good deeds and to be constant in prayer and almsgiving (21:73) this has the effect of further increasing the mercy God gives to his believers (19:78).

God's mercy is most evident in the guidance given through the revelations of the Qur'an and consequently is most available to believers. The mercy of Allah is seen most clearly in his forgiveness. Miller finds that forgiveness (*maghfir, ghufran*) in the Qur'an is essentially a negative concept and consists in not punishing, especially on the Day of Judgement. As salvation in Islam is essentially an escape from Hell to Paradise, so also the mercy and forgiveness of Allah focus on the remission of punishment that allows for this escape. Muslims who adopt this approach to salvation trust that on the last Day of Judgement Allah will indeed be merciful and compassionate. Hadith are also cited to support this view of Allah as the merciful one. Abu David is reported to have said, "God is more merciful towards his servants than the mother of the young birds to her young."[50] Abu Hurairah reports that Muhammad said, "When God completed the work of creation He wrote a book which is with Him above His throne ... Verily mercy outruns His anger."[51] Following the many references to God's mercy and these Hadith traditions has led many Muslims to trust in God's mercy as their way to salvation.

Salvation as the reward of faith

Many Muslims believe that salvation is the reward of faith. But what does faith require? The profession "There is no deity but Allah, and Muhammad is the messenger of Allah" is the content of saving faith to which one must assent with the mind, believe with the heart, and confess with the tongue. The emphasis upon intellectual assent is not meant to suggest that good works are unimportant. But as Qur'an 57:28 makes clear it is faith that makes a person a Muslim and eligible for Paradise: "O ye who believe, be mindful of your duty to Allah and put faith in His messenger; He will give you twofold of His mercy and will appoint for you a light wherein ye shall walk in, and will forgive you."[52] In Muslim thought the prophet

Abraham was taken as the model of faith to be emulated. His faith was regarded as an act of judgement by which something is held to be true. The word for faith, *iman*, literally means "trust," but faith was also taken to mean *tasdiq* or intellectual assent to certain propositions. Al-Nasafi, in his creed, "said that belief is assent, assent to that which the prophet brought from Allah, and the confession of it."[53] The great Muslim thinker al-Ghazali equated faith with "surrender and submission." Since his day the general view is that there is no difference between "faith" and "Islam." For example, according to Miller, the commentator al-Taftazani said that "belief and Islam are one, for Islam means resignation and submission, the acceptance and acknowledging of judgments, which is the real essence of assent."[54] As to what is the essence of assent, both the Qur'an and Hadith are clear that assent must be given to the message of the prophet Muhammad and especially to his doctrine of God. The required elements of faith are listed in Qur'an 2:177, "Righteous is he who believes in Allah and the last day and the angels and the scripture and the prophets."[55] All of this, however, is taken to be summarized in the simple profession, "There is no God but Allah, and Muhammad is his Prophet."

Although this approach to salvation through faith seems clear and straightforward, disputes developed over the essential content of faith. The Mutazilites, for example, held that faith is the knowledge of God that can be obtained through reason and the understanding of first principles. Al-Ash'ari allowed for varieties of faith including: belief in God, his prophets, and his revelation; belief in the Prophet's message partly in outline, partly in detail; or in knowledge of the Creator. Al-Bajuri said, "Faith is the inner assent given to the Prophet of Islam, to that which he has brought and to that which he has taught concerning religion. It involves obedience and submission to the message of the Prophet, he who is the true witness to Allah's revelation."[56] In all of these discussions the consensus was that saving faith required assent to Allah as the true God and Muhammad as his true Prophet. In the eyes of many Muslims this kind of faith brings salvation as its reward no matter what else a person may say or do. There is an understanding that unless there are exceptional circumstances such as a time of persecution, some sort of public declaration of one's faith statement is required. In times of persecution faith assent may be taken as a matter of the heart. In another context a person who confessed the basic Muslim creed on his or her deathbed was recognized as a believer and considered to be saved.[57]

The concept of becoming a Muslim by faith merges with the idea of becoming a member of the sacred community of Islam, the *Umma*. As Miller puts it: to have faith means to be a Muslim, to be a Muslim means to be a member of God's chosen community, and as a member of God's chosen community, you have the opportunity to receive God's guidance and forgiveness. Therefore, it is essential to be a member of the *Umma*, the Muslim community even if one's membership is rather nominal. "Taken literally it implies that everyone who is a Muslim will be saved, even though some may experience penalties for their sins."[58] The identification of faith and salvation with the *Umma* makes sense if one sees the community of Islam as the embodiment of the belief in God and practice of the Prophet as presented in the Qur'an.

Salvation through faith and works combined

An increasing number of Muslims argue that while faith is a basic requirement that cannot be dispensed with, alone it is not enough for salvation. Good works are also required, for salvation must be earned. Those who maintain this approach point to the many passages in the Qur'an where belief and good works are both required. For example, Qur'an 2:25: "And give glad tidings (O Muhammad) unto those who believe and do good works, that theirs are Gardens underneath which rivers flow." They also point to the Qur'anic teaching that on the Last Day, the activities of each person recorded in God's book will be weighed and judged. Consequently, there must be a union between faith (*iman*) and practice (*din*). Qur'an 2:172 details what is required:

> Righteous is the one who believes in God, and the last day and the angels and the book and the prophets, and who gives wealth for the love of Him to kindred and orphans and the poor and the son of the road and beggars and those in captivity, and who is steadfast in prayer and gives alms, and those who trust their covenant when they make a covenant, and the patient in poverty and distress and in time of salvation.[59]

Good works that are especially required of all Muslims include the five pillars of confession, prayer, fasting, almsgiving, and pilgrimage. The motive for good works is the fear of Allah who will judge one's good works on the Last Day, and decide if one is eligible for salvation. On the Day of Judgement one's sins will be added up by God and balanced off by one's good works. Sins are debts, as it were, and good works are credits. The credits must outweigh the debits, "Then for him whose scales are heavy (with good works) he will live a pleasant life" (101:71).[60] Thus in this view while faith is necessary, a person's relative happiness or woe after death is dependent on the good works accumulated in this life. One good work that automatically qualifies a Muslim for immediate entry into Paradise is the martyrdom of fighting and dying for Islam. In addition to the martyrs, the prophets and the companions of the prophets seem to be exceptions who will go straight to Heaven.[61]

The Hadith, or traditions about teachings by Muhammad and his first companions, strongly support the view that a Muslim may be justified by good works along with faith. For example, "It is reported from Abu Sa'idh-l-Khudri that the Apostle of God said, 'He who fasts one day in the road of God,

removes his face seventy years from the fire.'"[62] Again it is
reported by Abu Hurairah that Muhammad said, "The
completion of ablutions in a time of difficulty, and the going
a long distance to the mosques, and the waiting for another
prayer after the completion of one. This is protection for
you."[63] From both Qur'an and Hadith, this approach to
salvation is clear. Good works build up merit for the believing
Muslim. This also creates a disposition of heart and mind that
is pleasing to Allah. This combination of faith, works, and
submission to Allah is righteousness. But this righteousness is
never perfect, nor is it expected to be perfect. Humans, after all,
are weak because God has created them so. But if a person tries
hard to fulfill God's rules, given in the Qur'an, then one's
shortcomings and lapses are forgiven. Allah is merciful and
overlooks minor failings. "Thus by doing good works a
Muslim can outweigh and atone for his sins and can make
himself eligible for the mercy of God and His Paradise."[64]
However, in the view of orthodox theologians there is one sin
that excludes one from Paradise, namely *shirk*, or associating a
partner with God – an idea that combines polytheism and
idolatry. This is considered the greatest sin in Islam. It makes
one an unbeliever, or *kafir*, and bars one from Paradise. Other
sins do not make a Muslim an unbeliever but only a sinner.
"For great sins the Muslim sinner may have to spend a period
of purgative punishment in the Fire, but the fact that he had
faith means that he will eventually enter Paradise."[65] A
contemporary Muslim, M. A. Quasem of Indonesia summarizes this approach: "From the entry into Islam through
faith he [the believer] has to make progress and develop the
faith through action performed in the light of the Qur'an and
Tradition ... Thus faith and action taken together perfect the
life and bring about salvation."[66]

Salvation through intercession of the prophets

Intercession is also suggested as a means of salvation by many Muslims. "Since human sinfulness is universal and since God's decisions are unknown, and since it is not clear whether one's own works are sufficient to blot out one's misdeeds, the idea of a helper has been welcomed by some Muslims."[67] This notion developed even though the Qur'an clearly speaks against it. Qur'an 82:19, for example, says that the Day of Judgement is "a day on which no soul hath power for any (other) soul. The [absolute] command on that day is Allah's."[68] Other passages, however, seem to leave room for a future intercession. Qur'an 19:90 reads, "None shall have the power to intercede, save he who hath received permission at the hands of God's mercy." And Qur'an 43:86 suggests that those who truly witnessed to Allah may intercede to help others.[69]

The combination of human need and the positive passages in the Qur'an allowed the doctrine of intercession by the prophets to develop soon after the death of Muhammad. It offered hope to the sincere believer in the face of the uncertainty created by the doctrine of God's predestination. Unsure as to whether the worth of one's actions would modify the fate that God had preordained, the believer could take refuge in the hope that the intercession of Muhammad would evoke God's mercy and tip the balance in favour of salvation. The orthodox theologians struggled with the idea but accepted it on the basis of positive passages in the Qur'an. They also reasoned "that if pardon and forgiveness are possible without intercession, how much more permissible are they with it."[70] It is not surprising that Muhammad became the main mediator, although the possibility of others was allowed. Hadith supported this development especially with regard to great sins which could not be wiped out by good actions alone. So it is reported in Al-Tirmidhi's book of Hadith by Anas that Muhammad said, "My intercession is for those of my followers who commit mortal sins."[71]

There is also a tradition of Muhammad saying that on the day of resurrection he would fall down in prostration and intercession before God, who would accept the Prophet's requests up to a limit. In this way Muhammad will be able to bring out of the fire and into Paradise all except those for whom eternal punishment is proper.[72]

Shi'ite Muslims, a separate group from the orthodox or Sunni Muslims, have carried the idea of intercession much further, extending it from Muhammad to include his grandson Husain. Their thinking is summarized by Miller as follows:

> Shi'ites believe that when Husain, the grandson of Muhammad, died in the battle of Kerbelo ... he died for the sins of Islam ... They believe that at the resurrection Husain will rise with the intercessory power he has purchased with his blood. According to a tradition Husain says: "All rational creatures, men and jinn [spirits], who inhabit the present and future world, are sunk in sin and have but one Husain to save them." So the Shi'ites have Muhammad as the special mediator for the community of Islam and Husain as the "self-renouncing redeemer." But not only that, according to the Shi'ites their Imams, the eleven leaders who followed Husain, have the same power of mediation, and without their intercession it is impossible for men to avoid the punishment of God.[73]

Within Islam it is the Shi'ite community that has pushed the idea of salvation by intercession to its most extreme form.

Yet another approach is found in the popular idea that living Muslims can become intercessors for their deceased fellow believers. These prayers, often said over the bier of the dead, together with almsgiving on behalf of the dead, are held by many to be efficacious. The theologian Al-Taftazani approves of the practice and quotes a Hadith: "The prophet said, 'No group of Muslims amounting to a hundred in number, performs worship over a dead person, all of them interceding for him, without their intercession being welcome.'"[74]

In a variety of ways the practice of intercession has developed through the years into a popular means to salvation for Muslims throughout the world. Through prayer one gains forgiveness for sins from God. Prayer in its most universal intercessory form is seen in the idea that on the Day of Judgement Muhammad will plead for his followers like a lawyer pleads for his or her clients. "Some traditions [also] say that the Prophet will take the hands of believers and will lead them across the narrow bridge that separates heaven and hell."[75]

Salvation via the Sufi mystical path

The Sufi approach not only offers a different means or method for the achievement of salvation but also a different vision as to what that goal is. For the Sufi, salvation is not Paradise as usually described but rather it is a union with God which can be realized in this life. The means to effect this closest possible relationship with God are found in the Sufi spiritual discipline. With the guidance of a Sufi master, the devotee goes through a series of stages and states that culminate in spiritual union with God. Miller quotes Syed Hossein Nasr's description of that state:

> [It] means to be already resurrected in God while in this life and to see God "wherever one turns" ... He who has gained such knowledge through the means made available in the Islamic tradition and by virtue of the grace issuing from His names experiences God as at once transcendent and immanent, as before all things and after all things, as both the Inward and the Outward. He sees God everywhere ... having died to his passionate self. Through his death he has gained access to the world of the spirit and come to know His Lord, thereby fulfilling the goal of creation and the purpose of Qur'anic Revelation, which is none other than to enable man to know and love God and to obey His Will during this earthly journey.[76]

Annemarie Schimmel describes the practice necessary for such a state of mystical union in the life of Hwaga Mir Dard of Delhi

(1721–85).[77] Son of the Sufi Master Muhammad Nasr, Dard became his father's disciple at age thirteen. The spiritual practice Dard learned from his father was ascetic in nature and focused on the five pillars of Islam, especially prayer and fasting. Most important was ritual prayer and his fasting took an extreme form extending at times to twenty-one days and nights without interruption.[78] In the Sufi approach eating, drinking, and dressing are subject to detailed rules. Perfect trust and complete surrender to God is required from the disciple, rather than the joyful expansion of the self. Patience and gratitude are the required states of mind if salvation is to be realized. Another key requirement of the mystical path is frequent conversation with one's spiritual master. The result of the journey of devotions and recollections of the master's teaching "is that one's heart becomes free from all besides God, and is made ready for constant presence and vision."[79] In the Sufi tradition the way to God's presence and vision is through reciting the divine names morning and evening and meditating on their meanings. For example, says Dard, "when one says *la ilaha illa Allah* – There is no deity save God – one should think in one's heart *la ma' bud illa Allah* – There is no object of worship save Him – and *la maqsud illa Allah* – There is no object of desire save Him ... and the most innermost of the innermost is *la maqsud illa Allah* – There is nothing existent save God."[80] All the divine names point to the mystical experience of unity with God.

According to Dard, meditation on the divine names is the centre of religious life and leads to God's presence and vision. Dard's father, his spiritual master, describes this state: "He sees the blessed figure of the word *Allah* in the colour of light written on the tablet of his heart and the mirror of his imagination ... and will find God as the Surrounding, and himself as the surrounded one."[81] In this experience the symbolism of light, central to the Sufi mystics, becomes key – but is too complex to include in this brief description.[82]

Although Dard realized such mystical states he never ceased relying upon the acts of worship as absolutely necessary for salvation, and constantly asked forgiveness. Schimmel summarizes, "his whole religious system of reflection on the divine names, all his theories of recollection and contemplation, and likewise his overwhelming experiences on the Path, of which he was so proud, are summed up in the humble prayer for salvation through grace: 'My request is only that the king-bird [huma] of happiness, namely of being accepted by Thee, may open his wings upon me.'"[83]

In concluding his analysis of the means of salvation Miller notes that in the midst of their busy worldly lives most ordinary Muslims look to membership in the *Umma*, the Muslim community, as a sufficient hope. In popular Islam emphasis is placed on the intercession of the prophets, while Shi'i Muslims look to the intervention of their Imams. Increasingly, he suggests, ordinary Muslims place their trust in a combination of the mercy of God, and faith and works. However, thoughts and feelings about the various ways to salvation are still evolving.[84] Much clearer is the Muslim vision of Heaven and Hell.

SALVATION AND THE AFTERLIFE

The Muslim view of salvation and life after death is very graphically conveyed in terms of Heaven and Hell. But before reaching Heaven or Hell comes one's encounter with death. Although the Qur'an has little to say about funerals, guidelines for the burial of the dead were developed by scholars from the Hadith. The dying person is to be reminded of the primary statement of faith with "There is no deity other than Allah and Muhammad is God's Prophet" (the *shahada*) being whispered in his or her ear. The dead person is placed on a stretcher with the head in the direction of Mecca. Kassis comments, "It is as if dying is an act of prayer with the rituals of prayer being applied."[85] The mourners implore God to make the dying person's passage easy. Death is followed by *ghusl*, or ritual washing of the body. The body is then wrapped in a simple white cloth in preparation for a burial which, according to Hadith, should take place before night on the day of death or, if late, the following day. The body is carried on an open bier to the cemetery in a funeral procession which is to avoid displays of loud lamentation. All debts owed by the deceased are to be settled before prayers are said at the tomb. No prayers are said over the tomb of an unbeliever or a person who committed suicide. Nor are they required in the case of a martyr or a stillborn baby. Prayers include the saying of "God is Great" (*Allahu akbar*) four times with hands raised high, punctuated with readings from the Qur'an, intercession for the deceased and supplication for those attending the funeral. Burial takes place immediately after the prayers and without a coffin. As the body is placed in the grave the clothes are loosened, the face is turned toward Mecca and the *shahada* is whispered once more in the ear of the deceased. Then earth is placed loosely over the body and those in attendance individually say a prayer for the forgiveness of the sins of the deceased.[86]

In Islam the belief developed that judgement begins in the tomb shortly after death. The deceased is visited by two angels who make the dead person sit up in the grave (thus the loose clothes and loose dirt) to answer questions of the faith. If the person answers correctly about the oneness of God and the identity of Muhammad, he or she is left alone until the resurrection of the dead and the Day of Judgement. But if incorrect answers are given two angels will smite the person's face and back saying, "Taste the punishment of burning" (Qur'an 8:50) – this punishment is called the "torment in the tomb."[87] Thus in Islam we find the notion of a twofold punishment, the first of which takes place in the tomb. The second punishment comes with the Day of Resurrection and Judgement, which will usher in life after death.

According to the Qur'an, the Day of Resurrection is the time (known only to God) at which life on earth will end (Qur'an 33:63). It will be a time of terrifying events: the moon will split, there will be earthquakes, mothers will neglect their children and people will seem drunk even though they are not (Qur'an 22:1–2). Perhaps borrowing from Christian imagery, Muslim thought pictures a battle between Satan, who is attempting to lure Muslims away, and Jesus the Messiah, who will return with a spear in his hand and destroy the anti-Christ. This victory will be followed by two blasts of the trumpet. "Following the first blast and in preparation for the Resurrection, all living things will die. An interval will precede the sounding of the second blast of the Trumpet, at which all the dead will be brought back to life and assembled in preparation for the Judgement."[88] According to the Qur'an, judgement is individual. Each person will stand before God to answer for his or her actions (Qur'an 6:30), and God will ask each to read his or her own record (Qur'an 17:13–14). As they render the account of their actions, they shall be weighed in the cosmic scales:

> Then he whose scales are heavy – they are the prosperers, and he whose scales are light – they have lost their souls in Gehenna dwelling forever, the Fire smiting their faces (Qur'an 23:102–104).[89]

As we have seen above some passages of the Qur'an and Hadith allow for intercession by the prophets, particularly Muhammad – but intercession will not help anyone who has associated another god with God. Kassis notes that Hadith "preserves an image of a basin (hawd) at which Muhammad will assemble his community in the hope for admission to Paradise. The poor and those who were denied the comforts of the earthly life shall be in the first ranks."[90] However, Muhammad will be told by God that he does not know what his followers have done since his death, leaving the believer with a sense of mystery.

When it comes to Heaven and Hell the Qur'an offers very vivid and realistic descriptions. Muslims have debated whether to take these descriptions literally or to interpret them metaphorically. Miller observes that "Many Muslims, including Al-Ghazali, take the view that both the physical and the spiritual meanings must be accepted, the latter being the higher experience."[91] Some argue that the rather sensual descriptions of Paradise must be accepted just as they are, while others take them to be allegories of the blessings of heaven. The Hadith carry forward and further embellish the already graphic Qur'anic descriptions of Heaven and Hell.

Regarding Hell the Qur'an suggests that those failing to receive intercession, the wicked, shall be marched along the "Path of Hell," to the burning Fire: "Muster those who did evil, their wives, and that they were serving, apart from God, and guide them into the path of Hell!" (Qur'an 37:22–23). Hell is described as a burning fire into which sinners go, regretting their failure to heed the warnings given them:

> When they are cast into it ... it boils and wellnigh bursts asunder with rage. As often as a troop is cast into it, its keepers ask them, "Came there no warner to you?" They say, "Yes indeed, a warner came to us; but we cried lies saying, "God has not sent down anything; you are in great error." They also say, "If we had only heard, or had understood, we would not be inhabitants of the Blaze" (Qur'an 67:7–10).[92]

The Qur'an suggests that Hell has seven levels with different categories of people assigned to each level from the less severe to the most terrible as follows: unrepentant Muslims, Christians, Jews, and a range of idolaters with a bottomless pit for religious hypocrites. The overwhelming impression of hell is one of calamity[93] and raging fire (Qur'an 101:3,11).

When it comes to the righteous or those who repented and whose sins God has forgiven, they will be admitted to Heaven or Paradise. The Qur'an pictures Paradise as follows:

> Two Gardens, abounding in branches – therein two fountains
> of running water – therein of every fruit two kinds – reclining
> upon couches lined with brocade, the fruits of the gardens nigh
> to gather – therein maidens restraining their glances,
> untouched before them by any man or jinn – lovely as rubies,
> beautiful as coral. Shall the recompense of goodness be other
> than goodness? (Qur'an 55:48–60).[94]

The gardens of Paradise will be beautiful and its fortunate occupants will have all their wishes fulfilled. Rather than becoming too caught up into the material delights, the focus to be maintained is upon the mercy and compassion of God bestowed upon the faithful. The Qur'an in fact suggests that not material blessings but the vision of God will be the supreme good of Paradise (Qur'an 75:22).

Ordinary Muslims, says Miller, feel the issue of sin and salvation strongly, however, they may judge that to engage in too much discussion about it is fruitless. Rather, they realize that the final decision about their afterlife is in God's hands, but they think that their actions now can help to shape that outcome. So, in this life, they try to devote themselves to the actions that they know will please God.[95]

5

Hinduism

From the unreal lead me to the real!
From the darkness lead me to the light!
From death lead me to immortality!
Brhad, Aranyaka Upanisad 1.3.28[1]

This prayer from scripture contains the essence of the Hindu approach to salvation. The chief concern is for human life, which is capable of progressive development from present appearances to ultimate reality, from ignorance to illumination and from this limited life to eternity. Unlike Christianity there is no common creed that must be believed for one to be saved, unless it be that humans will be reborn over and over again until they reach perfection. And according to Hinduism there are a great variety of ways of being saved. Rather than sin being the major obstacle, it is ignorance that is the veil within our human nature that keeps us from realizing the divine. Ignorance (*avidya*), says Patanjali in his *Yoga Sutras*, is manifested in four ways: (1) in confusing the temporary with the eternal; (2) in identifying the impure with the pure; (3) in supposing there is joy in evil; and (4) in believing that the non-soul (i.e. the body) is the true self (*atman*). There is also the sense of egoism or "I-ness," which is inherent in all of us but which can be removed. Along with these go hatred or dislike and finally an attachment or clinging to life. Taken together these obstacles block us from seeing any life other than our everyday worldly and materialistic life and from realizing the fullness of life (*moksa* or salvation).

For Hinduism the fundamental question is what must I do or know in order to be saved? One of the appealing strengths of Hinduism is its great diversity of paths or *margas* to *moksa*.

The idea of a path to follow (*marga*) is central to the spiritual quest for Hindus. This quest is a search for reality, for understanding, and for timelessness. Gandhi caught the essence of Hinduism when he described himself as "a humble seeker after truth" and the Hindu Creed as "Search after Truth through non-violent means."[2] Rather than emphasizing doctrines to be believed, Hinduism focuses on the quest. Thus Hindus sometimes claim that Christians, Muslims, Jews, and Buddhists are actually Hindus in that they are all engaged in spiritual quests. Differences in beliefs, for example, about the nature of God, are of only secondary importance – since all are searching for the primary goal of salvation. "Hinduism is a process, not a result, of the Perfecting of Man."[3] The goal of the Hindu quest is no less than that the human should become divine. Indeed, in the Hindu view each of us will be reborn over and over until our quest, our path, or *marga*, finally succeeds in having us discover and realize the divine nature that is within. The gods cannot *become* divine for they already are. The lower animals do not have free will and the desire for release (*moksa*). Only humans have free choice and the conscious urge to expand their capacities without limit until their inherent divinity is realized. As we will see in each life humans are understood to be living under different capacities for spiritual development – differences they have created for themselves by their own exercise of free choice in previous lives. Different quests or paths to salvation are provided for people with differing temperaments and capacities. The generosity and attractiveness of Hinduism is that God's compassion, for those engaged in the spiritual search, reaches out with as many different paths as are needed to enable each person to reach release (*moksa*). And for the Hindu this *moksa* is not just the acceptance of a creed, performing rituals, or obedience to a code of ethics, although all of those are prerequisite requirements. Ultimately it is the direct living experience of realizing oneness with God that is the aim of the spiritual quest. But before focusing on this lofty goal let us begin by examining the condition from which each of us begins our search.

THE HUMAN CONDITION

For the Hindu it is not sin but ignorance that is the major obstacle to enlightenment or salvation. What is more we as humans have created this veil of ignorance that covers our consciousness by our own free actions. The basic Hindu explanation, called *karma-samsara*, runs as follows.[4] Every time you do an action or think a thought, a memory trace or karmic seed is laid down in the storehouse of your unconscious. There it sits waiting for circumstances conducive to it sprouting forth as an impulse, instinct, or predisposition to do the same action or think the same thought again in the future. Notice that the karmic impulse from the unconscious does not cause anything, it is not mechanistic in nature. Rather it simply predisposes you to do an action or think a thought. Room is left for the function of free will. Through the use of your free choice you decide either to go along with the karmic impulse, in which case it is reinforced and strengthened, or to say "no" and negate it, in which case its strength diminishes until it is finally removed from the unconscious. *Karmas* can be either good or bad. Good actions and thoughts lay down good karmic traces in the unconscious for the predisposing of future good karmic impulses. Evil actions and thoughts do the reverse. Scripture and tradition taken together distinguish between good and evil.

According to *karma* theory, all the impulses you are experiencing at this moment are resulting from actions and thoughts done in this life. But what if you experience an impulse, either good or evil, that seems completely out of character with the way you have lived since birth? That karmic impulse is arising from the action or thought you did in a previous life – which introduces the idea of *samsara* or rebirth. Your unconscious contains not only all the karmic traces from actions and thoughts done in this life, but also in the life before this and so on backwards infinitely, since in Hindu thought there is no absolute beginning. In reality, then, your unconscious is like a huge granary full of karmic seeds or memory traces that are constantly sprouting up, as conducive situations arise, impelling you toward good or evil actions or thoughts. Consequently, we constantly feel ourselves being pulled and pushed by our karmic desires. But the possibility of free choice always allows us to take control over these impulses.

Samsara provides us with the idea of a ladder of rebirth. At the bottom are the animals, in the middle are the humans, and at the top are the gods or divine beings (*devas*).

} gods, no free choice

} humans, free choice

} animals, no free choice

The "ladder" of *karma-samsara*

Assume that you are a human being. If in this life you use your free choice to act on the good karmic impulses and negate the evil ones, then at the end of this life you will have increased the number of good *karmas* and decreased the number of evil *karmas* in your unconscious. At death (where the *karmas* function like coins in a banker's balance) the increase in good *karmas* will automatically cause you to be reborn further up the ladder. If you repeat the same procedure of acting on the good and negating the evil over many lifetimes you will gradually spiral toward the top of the ladder and be reborn in the realm of the gods. Unlike humans, gods have no free choice, no power to act. All you can do is to enjoy the honor of being a god – of sitting in the mayor's chair for a day, as it were – until the merit built up from your good choices over countless lives is used up and you are reborn a human at the top of the human scale with the prospect of continued birth, death, and rebirth to look forward to. But what if in this life you used your free choice to go the opposite way – to act on the evil karmic impulses and to negate the good? Then at death you would have increased the number of bad *karmas*, reduced the number of good *karmas*, and automatically been reborn a step lower down the ladder. And if this negative pattern was repeated through many lifetimes you would spiral down and eventually be reborn as an animal. Animals are simply human beings in a different karmic form (which logically explains the Indian practice of vegetarianism – to eat an animal is to engage in cannibalism). Unlike humans, animals have no free choice. Their fate is to endure the sufferings that their instincts cause them. When they have suffered sufficiently to expiate or purge off the bad *karma* they built up through many lifetimes of making evil choices, they are then reborn as human beings with free choice and a chance to move up the ladder again through the process of birth, death, and rebirth.

When one thinks of this process as having been going on beginninglessly and sees the prospect of being born, growing old, dying, and being reborn apparently endlessly, the question comes to mind, "How can I get release (*moksa*)?" Hinduism gives one answer, Buddhism gives a different answer.

In Hinduism the thing that causes one to be reborn is the *karma* within one's own consciousness. The chanting of *mantras* is one of the most powerful practices for purging of *karmas*, and when the last *karma* is removed, *moksa* is realized. Although conceptualized differently by different Hindu schools, *moksa* may generally be thought of as the removal of *karmas* of ignorance that make us appear to be separate from *Brahman* (the Divine). When the last veiling or obstructing *karma* is removed, the fact that one is, and has always been, nothing but *Brahman* is revealed. That is *moksa* – the direct realization of one's own oneness with the Divine. In some Hindu traditions (e.g. the *Bhakti* or devotional paths) God's grace is relied upon to remove the final obscuring *karma*.

Another basic concept in the analysis of the human condition is understanding of the four stages of life: student, householder, forest dweller, holy wanderer. These four *asramas*, as they are called, provide a framework for the religious, psychological, and social needs of the individual from childhood to old age.

Each stage, ideally a twenty-five-year span, has its appropriate commitments and disciplines. Each span properly lived out will serve the human community and nurture the soul along the path leading to salvation or release.

The first stage is a period of celibacy and learning, of nurturing physical development, mental and spiritual health, strength and endurance. It is the *Brahmacarya asrama*, the student life, hinged, as its title suggests, on mastering the basic religious rituals and texts (learned by heart). There is no sexual activity at this stage as all one's energy is directed to study.

The second stage, *Grhastha asrama*, sees the individual take up all the duties, responsibilities, and opportunities of a householder, including getting a job, marrying, having children, and fulfilling community responsibilities. *Artha*, the pursuit of wealth, *kama*, the pursuit of legitimate desires, and *dharma*, the doing of religious and moral duties, are all appropriate goals for the householder stage of life. It is considered the key stage, for the householder is the "backbone" of Hindu community and supports persons in the other three stages.

When the primary responsibility of raising children has been properly discharged, the householder is freed from the immediate needs and interests of his family. When hair turns grey, skin wrinkles, and grandchildren arrive he may retire into the forest, the *Vanaprastha asrama*, with his wife. There they devote themselves to spiritual study and discipline under the guidance of a *guru*. While husband and wife may remain together, their relationship is purely Platonic, with no sexual activity – that is appropriate only to the householder stage.

The final stage of life is characterized by complete surrender, *Mahaprasthana*, the life of the recluse or holy wanderer. This period of life is devoted – with the support of the community – to meditation on the word of God and the practice of meditation. No longer is there special attachment to husband, wife, or children. It is not that affection for these is lessened or lost, but that all others are raised to the same level in one's love. All women are seen as one's mother, wife, or sister; all men as one's father, husband, or brother. As a holy wanderer (*sannyasin*) one is completely freed from restrictions of family, caste, and village loyalties, and instead is universally committed to love, teach, and help whomever one meets on life's path. In short, one has become a *guru*. As with the forest dweller, there is no sexual activity in this stage. It is at this stage of life that the goal of final release from rebirth (*moksa*) is sought.

The idea of the stages of life, the diagnosis of ordinary worldly life as obscured by karmic ignorance that hides from us the truth of our divine natures, and the provision by God of various paths to salvation or release – these ideas are all drawn from the Hindu scripture, the *Veda*, to which we will now turn.

SALVATION IN THE HINDU SCRIPTURES

The Hindu scriptures include a vast collection of sacred books commonly called the 'Veda'. A brief outline of this collection can be found in chapter 4 of my book *Scripture in the World Religions*.[5] We will sample some specific teachings on salvation, or release, found in the portions of the Veda called the *Upanisads* and the *Bhagavad Gita*.

For the Hindu, the spoken scripture of the tradition is the Divine Word (*Daivi Vak*) descending and disclosing itself to the sensitive soul. The "sensitive soul" was the seer, or *rsi*, who had purged himself of ignorance, rendering his consciousness transparent to the Divine Word. The *rsi* was not the author of the Vedic hymn but, rather, the seer (*drasta*) of an eternal, authorless truth. As the modern Hindu scholar Aurobindo Ghose explains, the language of the Veda is "a rhythm not composed by the intellect but heard, a Divine Word that came vibrating out of the Infinite to the inner audience of the man who had previously made himself fit for the impersonal knowledge."[6] The *rsi*'s initial vision is of the Veda as one, which is then broken down and spoken as the words and sentences of scripture. In this Vedic idea of revelation there is no suggestion of the miraculous or supernatural. The *rsi*, by the progressive purifying of consciousness through the disciplines of *Yoga*, had simply removed the mental obstructions to the revelation of the Divine Word. While the Divine Word is inherently present within the consciousness of all, it is the *rsis* who first reveal it and in so doing make it available to help all others achieve the same experience. The spoken Vedic words of the *rsis* act powerfully upon us to purify our consciousness and give to us that same full spiritual vision of the unitary Divine Word that the *rsi* first saw. This is the enlightenment experience of salvation or release (*moksa*), the purpose for which Hindu scripture exists.

In this enlightenment experience yet another difference may be seen: for most Hindus, once the direct experience of the Divine Word is realized, the manifested forms (i.e., the words and sentences of the Veda) are no longer required. The Vedic words and sentences function only as the "ladder" to raise one to the direct, intuitive experience of the complete Divine Word. Once the full enlightenment experience is achieved, the "ladder of scripture" is no longer needed. The very idea that scripture can be transcended is heresy to Jews, Christians, and Muslims. For them the obstructions of human limitations are such that even the most saintly person would get only part-way up the ladder; scripture (Torah, Bible, or Qur'an) could never be transcended in the sense that most Hindus accept.

Let us now sample some specific teachings on *moksa* or release from rebirth as found in the *Upanisads* (800–500 B.C.E.).[7] The concept of *moksa* is sometimes thought of as the ability to determine one's own actions. The *Chandogya Upanisad* tells of the learned Narada coming to Sanatkumara for instruction on the nature of *Brahman*. Sanatkumara asks Narada what he knows. Narada replies that he knows the four Vedas and the Puranas along with many other things. He also knows that he lacks the all important knowledge that will enable him to escape rebirth and realize release. Sanatkumara responds that Narada's problem is that what he has learned is the mere names of things. His knowledge is too shallow. While Narada's knowledge allows him to talk about many things, he is limited by the words he uses and does not know reality itself. "Is there more than name?" asks Narada. "Assuredly there is more than name," says Sanatkumara who then proceeds to lead Narada step by step into the full realization of the Self as *Brahman*: "The Soul (*Atman*), indeed, is below. The Soul is above. The Soul is to the west. The Soul is to the east. The Soul is to the south. The Soul is to the north. The Soul, indeed, is this whole world."[8] The one who fully understands this, says Sanatkumara, is self-ruled (*sva-raj*); the one who does not understand this is ruled by others (*anya-raj*). The former has freedom or release (*moksa*); the latter does not.

Narada's problem is that while he had much knowledge of the scriptural texts and could describe them in such detail that

he could pass difficult examinations, this descriptive knowledge – knowledge of "name and form" – did not release him
from rebirth. Indeed with much descriptive knowledge comes
the danger of self-conceit or scholarly pride. We think we
know a lot but the darkness of our intellectual conceit leaves
us worse off than the ignorance of those who trust in worldly
works. As the *Isa Upanisad* puts it, "Into blinding darkness
enter those who worship ignorance and those who delight in
knowledge enter into still greater darkness, as it were."[9]
Release cannot be obtained by the works, or material
possessions, of the world, although they are essential for the
householder stage. Only when one's householder duties to
family and society have been fulfilled is it acceptable to move
on to the spiritual life of the forest dweller. And even then one
must study the scripture with the correct motivation – not just
to know what the texts say, as Narada did, but to have the
direct experience of that to which they point as did the *rsis*.
The *Isa Upanisad* distinguishes between knowledge by
description and knowledge by acquaintance. I can describe
my wife in terms of her age, height, weight, color, her family,
and educational history, etc., but that is a very surface
descriptive knowledge when compared with the knowledge
I have of her as lover, when the two of us become as one. That
is knowledge by acquaintance or direct experience – knowledge that can never be captured in words. A Shakespearean
love sonnet may evoke it but not define it. Similarly with the
Upanisads, their aim is to move one beyond descriptions of
the essence of the world or of oneself to the direct experience
of it – an experience which brings release from karmic
ignorance and rebirth. So the *Mundaka Upanisad* states,
"This self [*atman*] cannot be attained by instruction nor by
intellectual power."[10] Rather, when one's thought is purified
and *karma* is purged off then one's Self (*atman*) shines forth.[11]
Then one has the direct realization of being one with *Brahman*
and is not reborn.[12]

It is important to understand this Upanisadic teaching about release (*moksa*) in the context of the stages of life described earlier. Hinduism is not a world-denying religion. Only when the responsibilities and joys of the student and householder or family stages have been fully enjoyed is one ready – if one has the deep desire – to move on to the final stages of seeking release from rebirth. One seeks to be freed from a worldly and sensuous life that has been tasted to the full and from the limitations of conceptual knowledge that leave one's deepest questions unanswered. There is also the matter of evil (*papa*) or sin (*papman*) which according to the *Chandogya Upanisad* is the final *karma* to be overcome before *moksa* is realized.[13] The *Upanisads* are not specific as to how sin and evil are to be shaken off but there are many references to cleansing via "fire." As the *Maitri Upanisad* puts it, it is the fire of *tapas* or intense meditation in the face of austerities that rapidly "burns off" one's accumulated sinful *karmas*.[14] Such a process, says the *Brhad-Aranyaka Upanisad*, consumes all one's evil until one becomes "clean and pure, ageless and immortal."[15] The evils from which one must be liberated are the imperfections of one's own physical, intellectual, and moral nature. Morality is required but, for *moksa*, much more than mere morality is needed. What is required is nothing less than a comprehensive vision of the whole rather than the part, and a spiritual discipline or pathway (*marga*) that makes the realization of all human potentialities possible.

The *Upanisads* offer a very optimistic view regarding the perfectibility of human nature. The goal of *moksa* is to become the perfect person that underneath the obscuring *karma* one already is. The goal of one's spiritual quest, which may extend over several lifetimes, is to find the *atman*, the true self within. Then the beginningless cycle of birth–death–rebirth (*karma-samsara*) will be ended and release realized. The *Brhad-Aranyaka Upanisad* tells of this quest for the self by Janaka, the king of Vedeha.[16] In dialogue with the *rsi* Yajnavalkya,

Janaka asks what is the light that will guide a person through the earthly journey? The light of the sun, replies Yajnavalkya. But what guides one when the sun sets, asks Janaka? The moon, replies the *rsi*, testing the seriousness of his pupil and then offering fire and speech as the next answers. But, responds Janaka, when the sun has set and the moon has set, and the fire has gone out, and speech is hushed, what light does a person then have for guidance? The Self or soul (*atman*) is the person's ultimate light, says Yajnavalkya, for with it one sits, moves around, does one's work and returns.[17] The *rsi* then leads Janaka into a deeper awareness of the Self (*atman*) by describing various psychological states in which it is experienced – first in dreams, then in deep dreamless sleep, and finally in death. But in none of these states is the self freed from its obscuring veil of *karma* and so it continually returns to worldly life. Throughout this dialogue with his teacher Yajnavalkya, Janaka, the king, offers the gift of a thousand cows for the answer that will set him free. Finally, Yajnavalkya describes the *atman* that is released from rebirth and again the king offers a thousand cows for that knowledge. The liberated Self or *atman*, says the *rsi*, is not this, it is not that (*neti, neti*), it is unseizable, it is indestructible, it does not attach itself, it is unbound, it is not injured, one sees everything as the *atman*. The moment of discovery finally arrives for Janaka when he realizes that this liberating knowledge is not something he can buy with gifts of cows or any other worldly wealth, but is an insight he must realize within himself. The "light-bulb" must go on within, as the cartoons depict it. The king must be ready to give himself up in order to realize his own release. His salvation rests in his own hands. It is nothing less than the realization that one's true inner Self (*atman*), for which one has been searching through many lifetimes is none other than *Brahman*, the Divine itself. As the great summary sentence (*Mahavakya*) of the *Upanisads* puts it "*Tat tvam asi,*" "That thou art." "That *Brahman*" that is the essence of the cosmos, "thou" (your *atman* or inner Self) "is." *Brahman = Atman.*[18] You, minus your karmic constructions of body/mind/ego, are nothing but *Brahman*. That, for the *Upanisads*, is the liberating knowledge, the "light-bulb" experience by which *moksa* is realized. The purpose of the philosophic dialogue between the *rsi* and the student leading up to the statement of the *Mahavakya* by the *rsi* is to systematically remove the obstructions of karmic ignorance in the mind of the student, which are preventing him or her from directly perceiving the Divine (*Brahman*). The systematic use of reasoning, in removing ignorance so that the immediate unshakable experience of *Brahman* can arise, is characteristic of the Upanisadic approach to the Divine. It is called the path of knowledge or the *jnana marga*. Various exegetical tactics are adopted by the Upanisadic *rsis* in their use of reasoning. One tactic is to seek to identify the essence of the empirical world with its underlying unity (e.g. *Mundaka Upanisad* 1.1.3). Another tactic is to raise the ultimate questions that seek to reveal the reality underlying all change and suffering (e.g. *Chandogya Upanisad* 6.2.1ff.). Perhaps the most difficult of these methods for the student is the wisdom required for the admission that one's own intellectual prowess and system-building achievements do not attain for one the Truth (e.g. *Katha Upanisad* 2.23). The use of the intellect will help by removing the obstructions of wrong ideas, but in the end all pride, even in such a meritorious achievement as knowledge of the *Veda* itself, must be overcome by spiritual and mental discipline so that the intuition of the Divine can occur (*Katha Upanisad* 6.10ff.). And in this direct vision, the Divine is found to be the overflowing of peace and bliss, or *ananda*, upon which all life depends (*Taittiriya Upanisad* 2.8–9).

To realize oneness with *Brahman* (*moksa*) does not mean going into some different state of being from what we are now; it means to enter into a fully perfected human life of eternal freedom. The *Bhagavad Gita* (150 B.C.E. – 250 C.E.) refers to it as *Brahman-nirvana* – a state of freedom to be experienced here and now, not in some after death time. Whereas the *Upanisads* focus on the path (*marga*) of thought or knowledge for realizing release, the *Gita* takes a more inclusive approach and identifies the additional paths of action, devotion, and discipline, each of which will also get one to *moksa*. And whereas in orthodox Hindu society, the Upanisadic path of knowledge (the *jnana marga*) was reserved for males of the upper three caste groups, the teaching of the *Gita* opened the way to salvation for all regardless of caste or gender. The path of action (*karma-marga*) requires that one do one's duty in society, whether that be as a homemaker, mother, nurse, carpenter, garbage collector, etc., with no thought for one's own fame, privilege, or financial reward, but simply as a dedication to the Lord. The intensity of that dedication will rapidly burn up one's obscuring *karma*, and when the last *karma* is removed by such dedicated service, *moksa*, oneness with *Brahman* is realized. As the *Gita* puts it, "work alone is your proper business, never the fruits it may produce."[19] All work, whatever one's job may be, is to be done in a spirit of sacrifice, never with any thought for personal gain. This is the path of *karma* for realizing release.

The path of devotion (*bhakti*), like the path of action, is described in the *Gita* as open to all regardless of sex or caste status in society. All that is required is the intense practice of daily devotion to the Lord in ritual service, songs of praise, or depth of prayer meditation. The intensity of this devotion together with the grace given by God will burn up one's obscuring *karma* and when the last *karma* is removed, release is realized. Nor is this response left solely up to our human effort, as was the case in the *Upanisads*. In the *Gita*, Lord Krishna is seen as an incarnation of the Divine who comes to earth to help humans achieve their goal of salvation or release. God's grace is given to the dedicated devotee in the form of help from Lord Krishna. As the *Gita* puts it,

But men intent on me
renounce all actions to me
and worship me, meditating
with singular devotion.
When they entrust reason to me,
Arjuna, I soon arise
to rescue them from the ocean
of death and rebirth.
Focus your mind on me,
let your understanding enter me;
then you will dwell
in me without doubt.[20]

The path of devotion (*bhakti marga*) introduced in the *Gita* is the one most followed by the masses of Hindus. Some suggest that it is the favored method of realizing release in the teachings of the *Gita*.[21]

The final path described in the *Gita* is that of *Yoga*, or self-discipline. It is a practical psychological technique of meditation that enables one to burn off *karma* and realize release. Yoga technique allows one to achieve the goals that are set forth in Hindu philosophy and religion. As the *Gita* puts it, "This wisdom has been revealed to you in theory; listen now to how it should be practiced."[22] It is this practice, in modified form, that has become popular throughout the world today, including sitting in the lotus position, controlling one's breathing and focusing one's senses for long periods of meditation. The classic statement of *Yoga* practice in Hinduism is found in Patanjali's *Yoga Sutras*, a text dated to about 200 C.E.[23] The *Gita* differs from Patanjali's presentation in seeing the true self within (the *purusa*) not as an independently existing entity but as a minute part of God. However, regardless of differences of theoretical understanding, the *Gita* agrees that disciplined Yogic meditation is yet another pathway or method by which one may obtain release. We will examine this approach along with the other *margas* of knowledge, action, and devotion in the next section. Commentaries and contemporary examples from each of these paths to salvation will be examined as they have been developed beyond the Hindu scriptures.

FOUR HINDU PATHS TO RELEASE (*MOKSA*)

Arising out of the scriptures of the Hindu tradition a great variety of philosophical and religious schools give further development to the ways to release of knowledge (*jnana marga*), action (*karma marga*), devotion (*bhakti marga*), and self-discipline (*yoga marga*).These developments were often fostered by major thinkers who composed commentaries expounding the seed ideas of, for example, the *Upanisads* and the *Bhagavad Gita*. Sometimes a path (e.g. the *bhakti marga*) was elaborated by the inspired singing of poet saints who attracted large followings. Master Yogis appeared pioneering spiritual disciplines of austerity that resulted in *ashrams* of devoted students. These and many other developments have continued to evolve in the living tradition of Hinduism right up to today. In what follows I will give a brief sampling of these developments following four paths that we noted above as present in Hindu scripture. In each case our survey will conclude with a contemporary example.

Jnana marga

As we have seen above the *Upanisads* are filled with teachings about ignorance and *moksa*. These teachings provided the basis for the use of knowledge as a pathway or means of reaching release from rebirth. But the *Upanisads* do not offer a consistent point of view. While they share common ideas there are also many conflicts. The basis for a unified path of knowledge was provided by Badarayana, who lived in the third or fourth century C.E. Known as the *vyasa*, or arranger, Badarayana selected and organized the key teachings of the *Upanisads* into a series of summary sentences known as *The*

Brahma Sutra or "the summary sentences about *Brahman.*"[24] These *sutras*, or summary sentences established the foundational basis for the *Jnana Marga*. But they did it in shorthand form, most probably for ease of memorization. It remained for commentators to draw out the meaning of these sentences. This they did, beginning with Sankara (788–820 C.E.) and continuing right up to the present day. But there is wide agreement that Sankara was the greatest. He was the founder of the Advaita Vedanta school that was directed chiefly against Buddhism – a movement that at the time was very widespread in India. He set for himself the goal of defeating Buddhism on two fronts, the practical and the theoretical. On the practical side much of the Buddhist success came from the monastic movement that the Buddha had pioneered and universities that had been established throughout India. To counter this, Sankara introduced the practice of Hindu monasteries to a tradition that had previously known only family worship and, in the last two stages of life, isolated holy wanderers (*sannyasin*). Following the Buddhist example, Sankara established communities of Hindu monks and located them strategically in, as it were, the four corners of India (Himalayas, Mysore, Gujarat, and Orissa). These four *mathas*, as Sankara called them, offered key locations from which the spread of Buddhism was effectively challenged.

But this organizational response would not have been successful without a knowledge content to teach. This Sankara developed by writing a commentary on Badarayana's summary sentences of the *Upanisads*,[25] along with other commentaries on the key Upanisadic texts themselves and the *Bhagavad Gita*. Sankara's *Advaita Vedanta* or non-dual teaching of the way to release runs as follows. The *Upanisads* teach us that ultimately there is only one reality, namely *Brahman*. Everything else that seems to be something different from *Brahman*, you, me, the world around us, is composed of the *karma* that covers and obscures our true self. Sankara calls this obscuring *karma*, maya, which he defines as neither real nor unreal but mysterious. It has the reality of a snake that one takes to be real when it is only a mistakenly perceived rope. Just as when one sees the rope clearly the illusion of snake vanishes forever, so also when we have a clear perception of the *Brahman* – the essence of each of us and the world around us – then the obscuring *maya* that has made us seem different from *Brahman* is seen to be ultimately unreal and disappears permanently. That is release, *moksa*. As to how one reaches this new awareness of one's true nature, Sankara begins by stating two prerequisite requirements. First, one must have fulfilled the ritual and moral requirements (*dharma*) to one's family and society. Second, one must have a burning desire to obtain release. Sankara's method is meditation on the *Mahavakyas*, or great sentences of the *Upanisads*, under the guidance of a *guru*, or teacher. Study of the *Upanisads* will gradually cancel out incorrect ideas of our true nature (e.g. that the real me is my body, my thought, etc.), as we saw above in the dialogue of King Janaka with his teacher Yajnavalkya. The student is moved step by step from thinking of reality as the world external to the body, then the senses and the mind, until finally it is shown to be nothing but the inner light of consciousness itself – *atman/Brahman*. Sankara's method is for the *guru* to patiently show the student the inadequacy of each incorrect perception of reality until the common kinds of ignorance about life, with which we all begin, are shown to be wrong – like the mistaking of rope for snake. This is like the *neti neti* (not that, not this) approach of the *Upanisads*. When, through this negation of wrong answers, the student's mind is almost fully cleared of obscuring incorrect ideas or *karmas*, the teacher, judging the time is right, says to the student *Tat Tvam Asi* – "That thou art" – or one of the other *Mahavakyas*. Hearing those words produces the final inner flash of insight, like the light-bulb-coming-on experience of the cartoon, which simultaneously cancels out the last remaining *karma*, leaving only the steady and continuous experience of *Brahman*. With the last *karma* removed so too is the cause of rebirth, and one is released from the cycle of *karma-samsara* (birth, death, and rebirth). *Moksa* is realized. For Sankara, the *Mahavakyas* of the *Upanisads* function as does light in a world of darkness. Once the light appears, the darkness disappears and reality stands revealed before us. *Brahman* has always been there as our true self, but obscured by the darkness of our karmic ignorance. The teaching of the *Upanisads* removes our misperceptions and in a final flash of insight, the inner light-bulb experience, we "see" revealed that we are, and always have been, nothing but *Brahman*, the only reality. *Moksa* is not something new but the revealing of what has always been there.

The *Jnana Marga* tradition systematized by Sankara has remained a vital way to release for philosophically minded Hindus right up to the present.[26] Buddhism virtually disappeared from India but Sankara's Advaita Vedanta school remains a potent force today in Hindu diaspora communities around the world. Two recent Advaita teachers are Vivekananda and Ramana. Swami Vivekananda (1863–1902) made Hinduism known to North Americans as an attractive alternative to Christianity in his speech at the Chicago World Parliament of Religions in 1893.[27] In a comparative study of Sankara and Vivekananda, Rambachan finds that Vivekananda significantly changed Sankara's presentation of Advaita.[28] Whereas for Sankara the Vedas (especially the *Upanisads*) were a source of valid knowledge or revelation without which release could not be realized, Vivekananda gave a higher place to *anubhava*, or the direct experience of *Brahman*, which he saw as the ultimately valid source of our knowledge of the divine. Scriptures like the *Upanisads* were only *provisionally* acceptable until verified by one's direct experience of *Brahman*. Vivekananda thus shifted the focus from the truth of the scriptures to the truth of direct experience as the criterion for one's saving knowledge of *Brahman*. This shift from objective scripture to inner experience, initiated by Vivekananda, has influenced most contemporary Advaita thinkers[29] and is in tune with the modern tendency to focus on the authority of subjective experience and downplay the authority of revealed texts.

Turning to our second contemporary exemplar of Advaita and Sankara, Ramana Maharshi (1879–1950), we find a similar emphasis on the primacy of direct experience. In fact Ramana had his own experience of self-realization without any role whatsoever being played by scripture. When he was seventeen Ramana was suddenly overcome by a feeling that he was going to die. Rather than look for a doctor he decided that he had to solve the problem himself. "With a view to finding out what it was that was mortal, he lay down and made his body stiff like a corpse. Then he realized suddenly that there was death only for the body and not for the Self, the 'I' within, which is deathless."[30] As Balasubramanian notes, Ramana had not yet been exposed to the *Upanisads* or the teachings of Sankara. He did not go through the traditional *Jnana Marga* pattern of disciplined scriptural study, rational reflection thereon, and repeated meditation until what I have called the "light-bulb" experience of oneness with *Brahman* occurred. Rather Ramana began at a very young age with the "light-bulb experience" and then went on to study the scriptural texts. As he put it,

> I had never heard of *Brahman*, *samsara*, and so forth. I did not know yet that there was an essence or impersonal Real underlying everything and that Isvara [the Lord] and I were both identical with it. Later . . . as I listened . . . to sacred books, I learnt all this and found that the books were analyzing and naming what I had felt intuitively without analysis or name.[31]

For Ramana, as for Vivekananda, the *anubhava* or Self-realization experience was primary; the scriptures were secondary. The role of sacred texts and philosophy is not to convey anything positive about reality or the divine but simply

to negate the false, which in ordinary life passes for reality. Like
the "not that, not this" (*neti, neti*) of the *Upanisad*,[32] the
purpose of Ramana's descriptive negation of ordinary thought
is designed to reveal the substratum that underlies all names
and forms. As Ramana says, "It underlies all limitations, being
itself limitless. It is not bound in any way. It underlies
unrealities, being itself Real. It is that which is ... It transcends
speech and is beyond description such as being or non-
being."[33] The major obstacle blocking this discovery is the I,
or ego, which takes itself to be necessary for realizing
knowledge. Ramana's claim, consistent with the *Upanisads*, is
that only when the ego and the "I-thought" is removed is the
veil of karmic ignorance lifted and the Self is able to shine of its
own accord. This is Self-realization or *moksa* – a state in which
"there is neither the mind nor the body; and in the absence of
the mind and the body, there is no such thing as the world. Such
a one has attained liberation."[34] The Self is not known in the
way that we know material objects – through our sense organs
and our mind. Unlike worldly objects, the Self is self-luminous
and reveals itself when the obscuring obstruction (e.g. the
karmic ego) is removed. This is the purpose of Ramana's
method of Self-inquiry. It calls for intense meditation in which
the mind counters its obsession with the objects of the world
and turns inward. Only a mind that is pure will turn inward
and this requires a diet of moderate amounts of pure vegetarian
food and fully moral conduct as prerequisites. As Ramana puts
it, "The mind turned outward results in thoughts and objects.
Turned inward it becomes itself, the Self."[35] The method of
Self-inquiry aims at the removal of the mind by discovering its
divine source. Ramana does acknowledge that there are other
methods for the removal of ego and the realization of release,
one of which is the path of love and devotion (*bhakti*) to which
we now turn.

Bhakti Marga

The focus in the path of *bhakti* or devotion is on the love and worship through which one purges off the obscuring *karma* and loses oneself in communion with the Lord. It is therefore a theistic path as opposed to the monism of the *Jnana* path. Unlike the monastic *ashrams* of Sankara, the devotional approach formed itself into theistic communities centered around manifestations of the divine in the form of gods such as Siva and Vishnu. Let us take as an example the Srivaisnava community of South India which worships the Lord Vishnu and his consort Sri and considers the theologian Ramanuja (1017–1137 C.E.) as its founding interpreter of scripture.[36] In addition to the Vedas, the epic poems of the *Bhagavad Gita* and the *Ramayana*, and the *Puranas*, the Srivaisnavas include some sacred texts written in Tamil composed by poet-saints who lived between the seventh and tenth centuries C.E., the *alvars*, who were immersed in the love of Lord Vishnu. The *alvars'* poems are filled with intense emotion and intellectual devotion, or *bhakti*, which includes the senses of belonging to, attachment, trust, homage, worship, faith, and love. "The *bhakti* of the *alvars* was manifested in ecstatic and ritual surrender to the Lord, singing the glory and majesty of the divine name, a sustained meditation on the divine attributes and service to the deity and other devotees."[37] In their interpretations of the founder Ramanuja's vision of how to reach salvation, the Srivaisnava community split into two groups – the Vadagalais (the Northern "monkey" school) and the Tengalais (the Southern "Cat" School). The distinction between the two schools is found in the difference in the degree of self-effort or God's grace required for one's surrender to the Lord and release from rebirth. Let us begin with Ramanuja's teachings and then examine the differences his followers introduced.

Ramanuja knew Sankara's teachings well and disagreed with them sharply. While Sankara may have helped revive

Hinduism in the face of the Buddhist challenge, Ramanuja saved Hinduism from becoming a "philosophers-only religion" and opened it to engage in the everyday experience of emotion and sense in the worship of God. Like Sankara, Ramanuja accepted that a person's *karma* was what bound them to a repeated cycle of birth, death, and rebirth. But unlike Sankara, who saw salvation as complete loss of identity in the oneness of *Brahman*'s pure consciousness, Ramanuja described release from rebirth as the human soul (*jiva*) serving the Lord Vishnu in an eternal state of communion and happiness. Like Sankara, Ramanuja established his position by writing an interpretation of Badarayana's summary sentences of the *Upanisads* along with commentaries on the *Gita* and *Upanisads*. But he also wrote on the *alvars* and gave more priority to the *Gita* than did Sankara. Ramanuja is the great systematizer of the *Bhakti Marga*. The prerequisites of the *Bhakti* path include performance of all the rituals and actions required by virtue of one's caste and stage in life, along with a systematic knowledge of Sanskrit scripture. This means that, at the start of its development, the *Bhakti Marga*, like the *Jnana Marga*, was restricted to men of the upper three classes of Hindu society – because women and the fourth class or caste group, the *sudras*, were prohibited from learning the Sanskrit Vedas.[38] But, as we shall see, Ramanuja, in his later writings, seems to have changed to a more open approach.

Following the *Bhagavad Gita*, Ramanuja says that *bhakti* is attained by intense love. Narayanan summarizes Ramanuja's commentary, "The devotee always remembers the divine names and seeks to worship and serve the Lord with joy. This loving activity is combined with a meditation on the Lord, a meditation filled with love and a realization of the knowledge that one is the slave or the 'owned-one' (*sesa*) of the Lord."[39] Ramanuja's image of God combines the *Advaita* or non-dual idea of one divine reality, *Brahman*, with the idea of God as the compassionate father, mother, lover, etc. The cosmos is God's body, of which we as individual souls (*jivas*) are parts, and the Lord is God's soul (e.g. Vishnu who incarnates as Lord Krishna). To obtain release we draw near to the Lord by our practice of devotion – the intensity of which burns up the *karmas* which are keeping us apart from God. As the *karmas* are "burned-up" by our devotion, we are drawn ever nearer until we are released into an eternal communion with the Lord – "communion" rather than "union" because our existence as a soul separate from the Lord but "one" within *Brahman* is retained. Just as the iron bar when placed in the blacksmith's fire eventually begins to glow and look indistinguishable from the flame, so also the devotee in intimate communion with the Lord gradually takes on the characteristics of the Lord's intense love until he or she appears as identical. Yet the soul (*jiva*) still retains its individuality.

For Ramanuja, the commitment of love, with which one turns from the world to the Lord, contains a strong sense of humility, trusting in the Lord as both a merciful father and a powerful sovereign. "One surrenders oneself to him because he is both mighty and compassionate (*Gita 9–34*), and these two aspects precipitate the faith, the confidence, the trust of the human being in the saving power of God and accelerate one's complete surrender."[40] Surrender, or taking refuge in the Lord (*prapatti*), is the essence of the *bhakti* path. It is through Self-surrender that karmic ignorance is removed and the clear grace (*prasada*) of the Lord is obtained. Ramanuja says, "the Lord out of 'loving grace' gives the understanding with which they can join him. Out of compassion alone he dispels the *karma* which is antagonistic to the *bhakta's* wisdom; for those whose thoughts are centered around him, for those who consign all their acts to him and contemplate him with devotion and worship, he becomes the saviour and delivers them from the ocean of life and death."[41]

Narayanan notes that under the influence of the Tamil poet-saints (*alvars*) and in his later hymns like the Hymn of Surrender (*Saranagati gadya*) – an apparent conversation between the goddess Sri, Ramanuja, and the Lord – or the *Sriranga gadya*, Ramanuja undergoes a change. Not as a leading scholar of the day, but rather as one who has no qualifications to reach the Lord, Ramanuja surrenders himself at the Lord's feet with intense meditation on the Lord as his only refuge. Ramanuja's final devotion and surrender rest on a promise of grace offered out of consideration for one's lowliness rather than for one's status and accomplishments. Salvation is assured to those who surrender themselves in their own weakness and seek refuge with the Lord. This opening of the Lord's compassion beyond the traditional boundaries of men of the upper three castes, Narayanan suggests, was the last word Ramanuja shared with his disciples. As evidence Narayanan cites Kurattalvan, Ramanuja's scribe and friend as saying: "Whatever one's caste, whoever the person, whatever his nature [the Lord] does not make a distinction if he has taken refuge at [His] feet. Such a person, the handsome Lord favours through his motherly affection."[42] Presumably this then opens the way to salvation for women and *sudras*, along with upper caste men who know the Sanskrit texts, so long as they confess themselves to be sinners, having no other refuge but the Lord's mercy. It is this important development that sows the seeds of division among Ramanuja's followers.

The Vadagalai, or Northern school, took *prapatti*, or surrender, as only one of several means to *moksa*, and only to be followed if one could not follow others. Some effort was required from the devotee rather than total reliance upon God's grace. It was thus popularly called the "monkey" school because the baby monkey must make some effort to cling to the mother, after which she does everything for the baby. This was seen as a metaphor of the relationship between the devotee and God for the Vadagalai school. *Prapatti* needed to be constantly practiced for the atonement of sins and the destruction of past *karma*. All persons could theoretically practice *prapatti* regardless of caste or sinfulness, but full *moksa* could not be achieved by one of lesser status than a Brahmin. This school traces its lineage back to Vedanta Desika (1268–1368).

The Tengalai, or Southern school, took *prapatti* as the only means to *moksa* and held that it was equally open to all regardless or race, sex, caste, or sinfulness. After the attainment of *moksa* no further practice of *prapatti* is required, although it may be done as an example for others to follow. Sin was seen simply as an occasion for God to give grace. Thus it was called the "Cat School." Just as the mother cat does everything for the kitten, so the devotee has simply to surrender and God's grace does everything else. Even the act of *prapatti* itself is made possible by the grace of the Lord. The Tengalai school traces itself back to Pillai Lokacarya (1264–1369) who said that because the human soul is "owned by the Lord, it cannot take the initiative in actively seeking the Lord's protection. But the human being is urged to turn towards the Lord" and give assent to the grace of the Lord. Then the person's sinful faults will be accepted as if they were virtues.[43]

Leaving the Srivaisnava tradition, we shift to a very recent teacher of the *Bhakti Marga*, namely Swami Bhaktivedanta (1896–1977), founder of the International Society for Krishna Consciousness (I.S.K.C.O.N.), which he brought from India to New York City in 1965. Swami Bhaktivedanta was initiated into the Gaudiya Vaisnava movement which traces its heritage from Caitanya (b. 1486 c.e.) and ultimately from Lord Krishna himself. Baird notes that Bhaktivedanta takes as his sources of authority the Vedic literature (including the *Gita* and *Puranas*) all of which is taken to be authored by Lord Krishna.[44] The human condition is that people, because of their karmic ignorance, are unaware that they are really part of God, and this is the cause of their personal and societal discontent. As Bhaktivedanta puts it, "Because of this lack of Krishna consciousness in human society, people are suffering terribly, being merged in an ocean of nescience and sense gratification."[45] Krishna created humans from his own nature and gave them free will which they have misused. Salvation requires that humans recover their forgotten true relationship to Krishna – thus Bhaktivedanta's slogan *Back to Godhead*, title of the I.S.K.C.O.N. magazine. Krishna's grace is there waiting, but it is the duty of the devotee to remove the obstacles to Krishna's grace so that Krishna consciousness will result. One must surrender and engage in devotional service which consists of nine different activities: hearing, chanting, remembering, serving, worshiping, praying, obeying, maintaining friendship, and surrendering everything. Through such service together with the mercy of the Lord, one's soul is cleansed of material karmic contamination and rises to the level of pure (*sattvic*) consciousness and then finally to Krishna's abode. Only the grace of the Godhead is powerful enough to "neutralize", as Bhaktivedanta put it, the sinful *karma* of the devotee and enable salvation to be realized.[46] The "Hare Krishna" or I.S.K.C.O.N. movement has had particular success in spreading the *Bhakti Marga* to many Europeans and North Americans. In addition it is now providing leadership in temples and worship for many Hindus in South Asian diaspora communities around the world.

Karma Marga

Karma Marga may be described as the path of unselfish action – of working without thought for fame or financial reward but simply as a dedication to the Lord. The foundational scripture for this teaching is *Bhagavad Gita* 2:47–48:

> Be intent on action,
> not on the fruits of action;
> avoid attraction to the fruits
> and attachment to inaction!
> Perform actions, firm in discipline,
> relinquishing attachment;
> be impartial to failure and success –
> this equanimity is called discipline.[47]

In this passage of the *Gita*, Lord Krishna is teaching Arjuna, the soldier and protagonist of the epic poem, that he must do his duty (*dharma*) and go into battle to protect others in society. But the key point of Krishna's teaching is his focus on the motivation behind one's action. People lacking in wisdom cling to the Vedic scriptures and do the prescribed rituals merely to gain pleasure or power for themselves. Arjuna, however, is to act not for personal gain but simply to do his duty. He is to give up attachment to the "fruits of action" or its opposite "attachment to inaction" (the attempt to live a life of contemplation without work). Maintain an equanimity of spirit regardless of success or failure, says Krishna, and get on with your work. The spiritual exercise of the soul is in working without thought that you will get some gain (fruit), for that is what keeps you in the karmic bondage of birth, death, and rebirth.[48] By doing one's daily duty with no thought for oneself but with intense dedication to the Lord, the intensity of one's dedication "burns-up" the obscuring *karmas* and when the last *karma* is burnt up, release (*moksa*) is realized. Ramanuja in his Commentary on these verses of the *Gita* says, action associated with fruits is bondage but action done for its own sake and in worship of the Lord becomes the means for salvation. All action belongs to the Lord. Do work thinking thus.[49] The renowned medieval commentator on the *Gita*, Jnaneshwar, adds, "Not by abstention from action does a man attain the state beyond *karma*, and not by renunciation alone does he approach perfection."[50]

Later, in chapter 3 of the *Gita*, the human dilemma is restated. However wise one may be or even if one withdraws from the world to sit in *Yoga*, one is still stuck with one's body, which requires us to act even if only for its own maintenance. Since, then, every person necessarily has to act, and since all action binds us to the world and its cycle of rebirth, how is one ever to win release (*moksa*)? Humans should imitate God, teaches the *Gita* (3:25), and do their duty in life – whatever it may be – in a totally detached spirit. The perfected person of action, like God, has nothing that needs to be done, but does his or her duty in life simply as a dedication to the Lord. Through the intensity of that dedication, one's *karma* is "burnt-up" and release is realized.

Many take Mahatma Gandhi to be a modern example of one who lived the *Karma Marga*. Certainly he was a man of action and called the *Gita* his "spiritual dictionary." In his Commentary Gandhi begins by noting that, like Arjuna, we cannot run away from our duty in life. No matter what, we are stuck with having to act. In Gandhi's commentary on *Gita* 2:47, the key passage teaching "desireless action," runs as follows:

> Your right is to work, and not to expect the fruit ... the reward of our work is entirely for [God] to give. Our duty is to pray to Him, and the best way we can do this is to work with the pickaxe, to remove scum from the river and to sweep clean our yards.[51]

The duty to society and the work of the lowly cleaner (called the "sweeper" in India) is picked out by Gandhi as an example of the kind of work that, if done as a dedication to God, will burn up *karma* and lead one to release. Gandhi incorporated this emphasis into his teaching that humans are equal even though their *varna*, or caste duties, seemed to make some higher and some lower. To counter this he claimed that all occupations were of equal worth, as were all caste groups – which he took to be the teaching about caste in the *Vedas*. To demonstrate this in his own life, Gandhi championed the cause of the untouchables, who were consigned the dirty jobs in Indian society (removing human waste, cleaning floors and toilets, tanning animal skins, etc.), by seeking to include them into the *sudra*, or servant class, renamed as Harijans (Children of God). In the early 1930s Gandhi dedicated himself to an all-India tour aimed at convincing caste Hindus to change their attitude and behaviour toward untouchables and low caste groups. Ambedkar, the

Untouchable leader of the day, sometimes supported but most often challenged Gandhi's attempt to change the behaviour of caste Hindus, which ultimately failed. Together, however, they managed to have the Congress outlaw untouchability in 1948.[52] However, many caste Hindus have been slow to embrace this change in their daily lives. In his leadership of India into Independence, Gandhi merged the principles of non-violence (*ahimsa*) and desireless or dedicated action into what he called *satyagraha* (truth force). By giving up one's own desires and dedicating one's non-violent protests against various forms of British injustice, Indians would succeed in driving the British from India and winning Independence.[53]

In Gandhi's view, for such "action campaigns" to succeed, they must be undertaken as a manifestation of spiritual discipline – as a dedication to God. Gandhi is a fine example of one who is dedicated to the path of salvation through action (*karma*). For a person, like Gandhi, with the temperament of always planning, practicing, completing, failing, and starting over again, the *Karma Marga* of dedication to desireless action offers an attractive path to release from rebirth (*moksa*). In moments of repose such a person gains strength and direction for more activity. One should do one's work in the world but not allow the world to possess one. One must reach a state of desireless action that allows one to attain a liberation that transcends all *karmas* and *dharmas* (duties). Rabindranath Tagore, the Nobel laureate, captured this approach well in this comment on the *Isa Upanisad*: "Do your work, but let not your work cling to you. For work expresses your life so long as it flows with it, but when it clings, then it impedes, and shows, not the life, but itself."[54]

Yoga Marga

Perhaps no other aspect of Indian culture is more widely known than *yoga*. In India thousands of self-styled *yogis* amaze the crowds of both locals and tourists with their "yogic" tricks. In the West *yoga* is a very popular word these days. From exercise programs to meditation training, *yoga* teachers abound in most communities of Europe and North America. And in bookstores, the self-help sections contain numerous *yoga* titles. In most cases these modern presentations of *yoga* are updated versions of some aspect of the *Yoga Sutras* of Patanjali (200 C.E.),[55] the great systematizer of the *Yoga* school. Pulling together seed ideas of *Yoga* found in the *Upanisads* and the theoretical thinking of the Sankhya philosophers,[56] Patanjali outlined a psychological and spiritual discipline that when rigorously practiced would lead to release. Key Commentaries filling out Patanjali's teaching were composed by Vyasa and Vacaspati Misra in the classical period shortly after the time of Patanjali and in the sixteenth century by Vijnanabhiksu. New Commentaries attempting to further develop *yoga* thought and practice continue to be written both in India and in the West. We will briefly examine one such contemporary presentation by Aurobindo Ghose at the end of this brief overview of the *Yoga Marga*.

Yoga starts with an analysis of ordinary experience. This is described as a sense of restlessness caused by the distracting influences of our desires. Peace, purity of mind, and release comes only when the distractability of our natures is controlled by the radical step of purging the passions. But if these troublesome passions are to be purged, they must be fully exposed to view. In this respect, *Yoga* predated Freud by several hundred years in the analysis of the unconscious. In the *Yoga* view, the sources of our troubles are the karmic seeds (memory traces) of past actions or thoughts heaped up in the storehouse of the unconscious, and tainted by ignorance, materialistic or sensuous desire, as well as the clinging to one's own ego.

At the ego awareness level of consciousness, *Yoga* conceives of human cognition on various levels. There is the function of the mind in integrating and coordinating the input of sensory impressions and the resurgent memories of past thoughts and actions (*samskaras*). These may all be thought of as "learned" if we use behaviouristic terminology. But, then there is the higher function of the mind in making discriminative decisions as to whether or not to act on the impulses that are constantly flooding one's awareness. This discriminative capacity (*buddhi*) is not learned, but is an innate aspect of our psyche and has the capacity to reveal our true nature. This occurs when, by our discriminative choices, we negate and root out the polluting passions (*klista karmas*) from our unconscious until it is totally purified of their distracting restlessness – their "pulling" and "pushing" of us in one direction and then another. Once this is achieved by disciplined self-effort, the level of egoic conscious-ness is transcended since the notion of ego, I or me, is also ultimately unreal. It is simply a by-product of our selfish desiring. Once the latter is rooted out, the former by necessity also disappears and the final level of human nature, pure or transcendent consciousness is all that remains.

According to *Yoga*, transcendent consciousness is not immaterial, but is composed of high quality, high energy luminous material (*sattvic citta*). Since all egoity has been overcome, there is no duality, no subject-object awareness, but only immediate intuition. All experience is transcendent of individuality. The subject-object duality is overcome by resolving all objectivity into an absolute subject (i.e. *Brahman*). *Yoga* psychology finds the essence of human nature to be at the transcendent level of consciousness, where ego and uncon-scious desires have been excised. Yogic meditation is a practical discipline or "therapy" for removing conscious and uncon-scious desires, along with the accompanying ego-sense, from the psyche.

For Patanjali there are five prerequisite practices and three ultimate practices. The prerequisite practices include: (1) self-restraints (*Yamas*: non-violence, truthfulness, non-stealing, celibacy, and absence of avarice) to get rid of bad habits; (2)

good habits (*niyamas*) to be instilled (washing of body and mind, contentment with whatever comes, equanimity in the face of life's trials, study and chanting of scriptures, meditation upon the Lord); (3) body postures (*asanas*), such as the lotus position, to keep the body controlled and motionless during meditation; (4) controlled deepening of respiration (*pranayama*) to calm the mind; and (5) keeping senses (e.g. sight, hearing, touch, etc.) from distracting one's mind (*pratyahara*) by focusing them on an object or point of meditation.

The ultimate practices are: (1) beginners spend brief periods of fixed concentration (*dharana*) upon an object (usually an image which represents an aspect of the divine that appeals to one, e.g. Isvara, Siva, Krishna, Kali); (2) as one becomes more expert, concentration upon the object is held for longer periods (*dhyana*) and the sense of subject-object separation begins to disappear from one's perception; (3) *samadhi* occurs when continuous meditation upon the object loses all sense of subject-object separation – a state of direct intuition or becoming one with the object is achieved.

Through these yogic practices one has weakened the hold of the egocentric memories and desires (*karmas*) from the conscious and unconscious levels of one's psyche, and the discovery of the true Self has begun. Four levels of *samadhi*, each more purified than the last, may be realized through repeated practice of yogic meditation. The final state (*nirvicara samadhi*) occurs when all obstructing ego desires have been purged from the psyche, which is now like a perfectly clear window to the aspect of the divine (e.g. Isvara, Siva) which has served as the object of meditation. According to the *Yoga Sutras*, any image will do. The divine image is only an instrument to aid in the direct experience of the transcendent – at which point the image is no longer needed. Meditation of the sort prescribed by the *Yoga Sutras* is esoteric in nature, requires the supervision of a teacher (*guru*) who has achieved perfection, and is a full-time occupation which, even in traditional India, was not possible for most people until the final stage of life – retirement from worldly affairs and withdrawal to a forest *ashram*.

One such *ashram* was established at Pondicherry, India, in the first half of the twentieth century by the contemporary Yogi Aurobindo Ghose (1872–1950 C.E.). Aurobindo, after studying Western psychology in England, revised *Yoga* thought and practice to include modern evolutionary theory while still remaining rooted in the *Veda*.[57] Through his major writings, such as *The Life Divine* and *The Synthesis of Yoga*, Aurobindo developed his own approach, which he called "Integral Yoga."

In Aurobindo's view human nature is at first entirely veiled by *karma*, but there is something within that survives death and draws the human in an upward evolution. *Yoga* practices foster this development but alone cannot bring about the total transformation needed. For that to happen another power is required which Aurobindo calls the Supermind. Only the Supermind, described as "self-achieving Truth-Consciousness," can descend without losing its full power of action and help us to achieve our upwards spiritual evolution. As Aurobindo puts it, "For a real transformation there must be direct and unveiled intervention from above; there would be necessary, too, a total submission and surrender of the lower consciousness."[58] Aurobindo's system of *Integral Yoga* is complex and difficult to summarize. It is a theory of not just individual but cosmic salvation in which the paths to union with *Brahman* are two-way streets: Enlightenment comes from above while the spiritual mind, through yogic practice, strives to reach upward from below. When these two meet an illumination arises that transcends both reason and intuition, and eventually frees the individual from the karmic bonds of individuality – and by extension all humankind – to *moksa*. Thus Aurobindo's *Yoga* looks to a future evolution of consciousness that offers salvation to both individuals and all humans. Aurobindo attempted to express this complex vision through philosophical writings, plays, poetry, and the creation of a model spiritual community, Auroville, which attracted many devotees from the West.

The above four *Margas*, or paths to release, represent the dominant Hindu thinking on salvation and how to reach it. Unlike Judaism, Christianity, and Islam, not a lot of attention is given to Heaven or the afterlife since in the Hindu view the afterlife is composed of being reborn on earth over and over again until, through the practice of one of the above *Margas* the obscuring *karma* is purged off and release is realized. This is salvation and it will occur during life on earth (*jivanmukti*), after which one will not be reborn on earth but will enjoy eternal union or communion with the divine.

6

Buddhism

> Even as, monks, the mighty ocean has but one taste, the
> taste of salt, in the same way, monks, this teaching and
> discipline has but one taste, the taste of liberation.
>
> *Udana* 5.5[1]

With these words Gotama Buddha (*c.* 563–483 B.C.E.) describes
to the monks who follow him, his teaching on salvation
(liberation from suffering and rebirth). Ancient India, where
the Buddha lived, was a land of large rivers, sometimes these
could be crossed by boats but at other times, when the flow
slackened, they had to be forded on foot. Crossing over such
rivers was a major challenge for travelers and became a
common metaphor for salvation in Buddhism. One of the titles
given to the Buddha was that of "one who has crossed over the
difficult current of suffering and rebirth, and shown a way for
others to follow." It is a metaphor for escape from the miseries
of *karma-samsara* (the "current" of birth, death, and rebirth),
to the far shore of freedom, or release (*nirvana*). The term
nirvana literally means the blowing out of a candle flame – in
this case the "flame" of ego-selfish karmic desires that cause
one to be trapped in the suffering of *karma-samsara*. To achieve
this escape Buddhists speak of taking refuge in the Three

Jewels: the Buddha, the *Dharma* (his teaching), and the *Sangha* (the monastic community he established). The taking of these "Refuges" is what defines a person as Buddhist.

When they speak of taking refuge in the Buddha, Buddhists are thinking of Gotama Buddha (Buddha is a title meaning "the Enlightened or Awakened One"). Gotama is the family name of a man who was born in the foothills of the Himalayas as the son of a father who ruled a small kingdom in Hindu society. Tradition has it that Gotama was married at a young age and had a son, but left home at age twenty-nine to find a new answer as to how to find release from suffering and rebirth (he did not find the Hindu answer satisfactory). After much rigorous trial and error, he reached enlightenment at age thirty-five while seated in meditation beneath a tree, at Bodh Gaya in North India, by realizing the truth (*Dharma*). For Buddhists (as we saw for Hindus) truth is eternal but is blocked from realization by the *karma* we created for ourselves through actions and thoughts in this and previous births. The cosmos has no beginning but goes through vast cycles. From time to time there arises a religious genius, a Buddha, who has purified himself of obscuring *karma*, has "seen" the truth, or *Dharma*, and out of divine compassion teaches it to others so that they too may obtain Enlightenment, or release from suffering and rebirth. Buddhists think of Gotama as the most recent teacher in an infinite series of Buddhas. Gotama claimed to be only a human being, having no special inspiration from any god. As Rahula puts it, "He attributed all his realization, attainments, and achievements to human endeavor and human intelligence. A man and only a man can become a Buddha. Every man has within himself the potentiality of becoming a Buddha."[2] Buddhist salvation is open to anyone willing to follow the Buddha's example and strive for it. Why then is it so difficult? What is the Buddha's analysis of the sinfulness that is holding us back?

THE HUMAN CONDITION

In his analysis of the human condition, Buddha adopted the same starting point that Hindus assumed – namely that each of us is obscured by ignorance that results from the *karma* created by freely chosen actions and thoughts (especially our intentions) in this and previous lives. This *karma*, which we have created for ourselves, is stored up in our unconscious and acts as a veil of ignorance which keeps us from seeing the truth. It is this *karma* that causes us to be reborn and to repeat the beginningless and seemingly endless cycle of birth, death, and rebirth. But the Buddha differs sharply from Hinduism in the answer he gives as to how to get release from *karma-samsara*, this cycle of birth, death, and rebirth. However, before focusing on the Buddha's answer, let us examine some points of emphasis in the analysis of the human condition that are unique to Buddhism.

First, based upon his own experience, the Buddha emphasized that each person has both the freedom and the responsibility to work out his or her own path to salvation, or release. Indeed, we will keep on being reborn until we do. But each of us has the power to liberate ourselves from ignorance and the suffering it causes us by our own personal effort and intelligence. Through the example of his own life the Buddha has shown us the way to liberation (*nirvana*), yet we must each tread the path for ourselves. Because of this emphasis on individual responsibility, the Buddha allows complete freedom to his followers. Nor did he try to control the *Sangha* (the Order of Monks and Nuns) or want the *Sangha* to depend on him. *Nirvana*, taught the Buddha, comes with our own realization of truth and does not depend on the grace of a god, nor is it a reward for good behaviour or the blind following of someone's teachings or scriptures as divine revelation. Therefore, one's search for the path to release should always begin with doubt, as did the experience of

Gotama in questioning the Hindu teaching within which he had been raised. The Buddha made this clear in his discussions with the inhabitants of the town of Kalama. They told the Buddha that they were left in doubt and perplexity by the differing claims to truth of visiting holy men and Hindu teachers (Brahmins). In his response the Buddha commended their doubt in the face of such conflicting claims:

> Yes, Kalamas, it is proper that you have doubt ... do not be led by reports, or tradition, or hearsay. Be not led by the authority of religious texts, nor by mere logic or inference, nor by considering appearances, nor by delight in speculative opinions ... nor by the idea: "this is our teacher." But, O Kalamas, when you know for yourselves that certain things are unwholesome and wrong ... then give them up ... And when you know for yourselves that certain things are wholesome and good, then accept them and follow them.[3]

The Buddha rigorously extended this principle of doubting any teaching or teacher by applying it to himself. His teaching should only be accepted and followed if it proved to be true and trustworthy when one tested it out for oneself. But to even "try out" the Buddha's teaching one must give it at least "provisional acceptance." It is rather like trying to find one's way to an address in a foreign city. One asks directions of a stranger who may reply, "Go three blocks straight ahead, at the stoplight turn right, pass three more traffic signals and it will be on your right." You follow these directions (give them "provisional trust") as long as they seem to be taking you to where you want to go. But if they do not prove out in experience you reject them as false and ask someone else for new directions or simply search out the address on your own. The spiritual quest is like that, said the Buddha, you have the freedom, responsibility, and intelligence to test out each proposed answer for yourself until the Truth reveals itself to you in your own "testing-out" experience. That was the way the Buddha reached his own enlightenment experience.

The fundamental characteristics of our ordinary human experience is that it is filled with ignorance and false views as to the truth. There is no sin in the sense of disobedience to God or to some blindly believed scripture. Rather, for Buddhism there is the karmic ignorance caused by the many false views that assail us on all sides. To overcome these false views one must begin by doubting them all. But one must not get trapped in doubt for that would be to give up the search for truth and end in nihilism. As Rahula puts it, "As long as there is doubt, perplexity, wavering, no progress is possible. It is also equally undeniable that there must be doubt as long as one does not understand or see clearly. But in order to progress further it is absolutely necessary to get rid of doubt. To get rid of doubt one has to see clearly."[4] To break out of this circle, one puts "provisional faith" in the Buddha and follows his teaching to see if it enables us to begin to see more clearly. Only if it does should one continue to follow it – but always testing it out as one goes. It was in this spirit of equally testing out all views that the Buddha exhibited an openness towards all other religions and their teachings – and urged his followers to do the same.

A second point of emphasis about our human condition is that the experience of being trapped by ignorance and within the confusion of conflicting views is one of *dukkha* – which in English includes suffering, frustration, and dissatisfaction. In his analysis of *dukkha* the Buddha is like a physician diagnosing a sickness from which we all suffer, although in our ordinary life we may not be aware that we are ill. The Buddha described the *dukkha* from which we all suffer in three ways.[5] First there is *dukkha* as ordinary suffering. This includes physical pain when we hurt ourselves, when a toothache starts or when we are physically sick. It also includes the aches and pains of arthritis or other ailments that assail us as we age. The pain involved in giving birth to a baby, in sickness and finally in death is an inescapable part of human experience. But this kind of ordinary physical pain is only the first kind of *dukkha*. The second, due to impermanence, is more psychological in nature and is characterized by feelings of frustration and unhappiness. This kind of *dukkha* occurs when an initial experience of pleasure changes to pain – as when we sit down to a banquet of delicious food and overeat ending up with a stomach ache because we have taken too much. In our everyday experience, taught the Buddha, pleasure is pain in the making. Pleasure is insatiable and therefore it always leaves a desire for more, which in itself is a kind of unquenchable pain. In sexual experience, for example, is one ever completely satisfied or sated so that no more sex is pursued – or is one always left wanting more? This lack of lasting happiness or satisfaction is a major part of *dukkha*. And when it comes to clothes, houses, cars, computers – material possessions – we can always think of something else we need before we will be satisfied. The neighborhood we live in changes over time in ways we don't like. Unpleasant people move in next door. In our personal relationships a loved one may get sick or die. At work, the job we enjoy may be taken away and a new one given that does not seem so pleasant. In these and many other ways our everyday life, when we stop to analyze it, is full of frustration – mental suffering or *dukkha*. A third kind of *dukkha* is caused by the drives, lusts, greed, etc. that lead one to acts and mental states that cause suffering. For example, we become angry with our lover, mother, child, or sister rupturing a relationship and leaving a deep unhappiness that fills our minds and hearts. Our selfish desires (karmic impulses) cause problems in our relationships with others, and even within ourselves leave us always wanting more or better than what we have.

With this diagnosis the Buddha leaves no doubt that our ordinary human condition is an existence filled with *dukkha* or suffering. The wise person recognizes this, the fool does not. Realization of this is the spiritual first step – the awareness that suffering (*dukkha*) is the universal human condition and that it cannot be cured by the world's medicine of wealth, fame, possessions, pills, etc. We may try all these usual ways of dealing with our mental frustrations and physical pains but eventually – even though it may take several lifetimes – we will get fed up with these alluring but ultimately false remedies and search for a new understanding that will take us out of this worldly ignorance and the seemingly endless suffering of birth, death, and rebirth. That is when we are ready to seriously consider the path to salvation or release from suffering (*nirvana*) taught by the Buddha. The Buddha's role as a saviour amounts to revealing the path and offering it to us. But then it is up to us. The way people respond divides them into two groups – the ordinary persons and those who become disciples (the *arya*). Buddhist scripture describes the ordinary person as the one who has not heard the Buddha's teaching or been changed by it, and identifies his self with an inner ego or soul. The other kind of person, the *arya* or disciple of the Buddha, recognizes *dukkha* or suffering for what it is and enters the path to release pioneered by the Buddha.[6] In Buddhist teaching much emphasis was put on changing from being an "ordinary person" satisfied with the everyday experience of the human condition to being an *arya*, one who is installed in the Buddha's family and whose eyes are being opened. Enlightenment or release from ignorance (*nirvana*) is described by the Buddha as like being "awakened" or "having one's eyes opened." Like the Hindu *moksa*, it is an experience of "inner intuition" of knowing by direct acquaintance rather than knowing by description.

In summary, the Buddha's diagnosis of the human sickness (karmic ignorance) in which we are all trapped through repeated rebirths is that it is composed of *dukkha* or suffering of two kinds: a) wanting things you don't have; and b) wanting to get rid of something you are currently stuck with, e.g. an unhappy marriage. It is our mental attitude, not the experience itself, that causes our sense of suffering – our desires, our anxieties. Nor should we think that science or technology will get us over our suffering. It may help to postpone disease but it cannot stop the process of aging and the ultimate prospect of death. The Buddha's prescription for this illness of human condition that we all experience is nothing less than a complete change in our mental attitude and our self-understanding that comes when our eyes are opened to the karmic ignorance of the false views in which we have lived for many lifetimes – and look to continue living for lifetimes into the future. This radical change in lifestyle and self-perception is available to all regardless of gender, age, caste group, or lifestage – educated or uneducated. This is a remarkable basis for religion in that it involves no authoritative scripture or doctrine, no divine grace, no dependence on a God or divine being. Salvation is realized simply by one's own effort. What the Buddha offers is a path, based on his own experience, that led him to enlightenment (*nirvana*) and that one can try out for oneself. This path is offered in his teaching of The Four Noble Truths and The Eightfold Noble Path that together form the foundation of Buddhist scripture.

SALVATION IN BUDDHIST SCRIPTURE

Buddhist scripture, the *Tripitaka* is composed of the *Sutras*, or Sayings of the Buddha; the *Vinaya*, or Rules for the Monasteries, established by the Buddha; and the *Abhidharma*, or Commentaries on the teachings of the Buddha, composed by Buddha's followers. Together these make up the Canon of Buddhist Scriptures as established by the monastic orders first in oral and later in written form following the Buddha's death. These scriptures are preserved in many different language collections including: Pali, Tibetan, and Chinese – with the Pali collection also available in Sanskrit. As mentioned above, scripture in Buddhism is not considered to be divine revelation but rather a human record of the Buddha's Enlightenment and the path to it for those who want to follow him. The Buddha's followers did split into various schools or denominations to which we will refer later. All schools accept a core collection of *Sutras* and *Vinaya* but differ in regard to the *Abhidharma*, with each school offering its own Commentaries as to the meaning of the Buddha's Sayings. The relation between the Buddhist scriptures and salvation for monks is well stated by the contemporary scholar Yun-Hua Jan:

> Through a regulated life in accordance with the *Vinaya* rules, to study doctrinal statements attributed to the Buddha as presented in the *sutras*, to practice the teaching and to reflect on some of the points in the light of the commentaries are the consistent directives in Buddhist tradition. It is only through the threefold effort, the religious goal of Buddhahood or *Nirvana* might be attainable.[7]

Rather than speaking in Sanskrit, the elite language of the Hindu brahmins and the Vedas, the Buddha taught in the language of the common people of his day. He made his teaching of the path to salvation open to all, regardless of caste or gender.

A study of the *Sutras*, or sayings, the original teachings of the Buddha, indicates that he had definite views regarding the Vedic revelation of the Hindus.[8] In the Buddha's view none of the teachers of the Hindu Vedic tradition, not even the original *rsis*, have experienced a direct vision of *Brahman*. Thus, the Vedic claim to scriptural knowledge of *Brahman* is not trustworthy because it is not founded on direct experience of *Brahman*. The Veda, therefore, cannot be accepted as a revelation of truth. In his own religious experience, Gautama rejected a faith acceptance of the Veda and went out in search of a direct personal experience of reality. The words he spoke, which became the Buddhist scriptures, were a description of his experience of striving for and finally achieving the state of *nirvana*. Having had the direct personal experience face to face as it were, the Buddha had none of the doubts that had worried him regarding the experience of the Hindu *rsis*. The words he spoke (e.g., "The Four Noble Truths") were intended to exhort and instruct others to enter this same path and also to realize release (*nirvana*). Buddha's followers judged him to speak with an authority that arose from his own enlightenment experience, yet there seemed to be no thought that his words represented divine revelation or that they were dictated by a god. Rather, as Lancaster puts it, his "teaching arose from insights achieved in a special state of development, a state open and available to all who have the ability and desire to carry out the tremendous effort needed to achieve it."[9] For Buddhism, as was the case for Hinduism, the truth taught by the scriptures is beginningless and eternal. Like the *rsis* (as they are understood within Hinduism), Gautama acts to clear away karmic obstructions that obscure the eternal truth. Other Buddhas have done this before him, and will do it again after him. Revelation in this Buddhist sense is *parivartina* – turning something over, explaining it, making plain the hidden. This is the role of the Buddhas: to make visible the timeless truth to the unenlightened; to point the way to *nirvana*. In the Buddhist view each of us is a potential *buddha* obscured in karmic ignorance, but with the possibility for enlightenment within. This the Buddha offers to us in his teaching of the Four Noble Truths.

Preached as the first teaching following his enlightenment experience on the outskirts of the city of Banaras, The Four Noble Truths are judged to contain the essence of the Buddha's vision of release. It is held to be a middle path between the extreme of luxury, on the one hand, and the extreme of asceticism on the other. This middle path is reflected in the *Vinaya*, the rules Buddha established for his monastic communities. The Four Noble Truths should be taken like the *Mahavakyas* or summary sentences of the *Upanisads*, not as the premises for a deductive system of logic or doctrine, but as teachings to be meditated upon until the learner, in a flash of insight (like the cartoon "light-bulb" experience), suddenly "catches on" and breaks through to another level of knowledge and experience. As, for example, in the Buddha saying while teaching, "so and so has caught on!" The Buddha's teaching of The Four Noble Truths is as follows:

> The First Noble Truth of suffering (*dukkha*) is this: Birth is suffering; aging is suffering; sickness is suffering; death is suffering; sorrow and lamentation, pain, grief, and despair are suffering; association with the unpleasant is suffering; dissociation from the pleasant is suffering; not to get what one wants is suffering – in brief, the five aggregates of attachment are suffering.
> The Second Noble Truth of the origin of suffering is this: It is this thirst (craving) which produces rebirth and re-becoming, bound up with passionate greed. It finds fresh delight now here and now there, namely, thirst for sense-pleasures; thirst for existence and becoming; and thirst for non-existence (self-annihilation) ...
> The Third Noble Truth is the Cessation of suffering (Nirvana) which we must realize.
> The Fourth Noble Truth is the Noble Eightfold Path leading to the realization of Nirvana: namely right view; right thought; right speech; right action; right livelihood; right effort; right mindfulness; right concentration.
> As long as my vision of true knowledge was not fully clear in these three aspects, in these twelve ways, regarding the Four Noble Truths, I did not claim to have realized the perfect Enlightenment ... But a vision of true knowledge arose in me thus: My heart's deliverance is unassailable. This is my last birth. Now there is no more re-becoming (rebirth).
> This the Blessed One said. The group of five bhikkhus was glad, and they rejoiced at his words.[10]

In the Buddha's teaching, thirst, craving, or desire is the key component of our *karma* that causes rebirth. By understanding and enacting his teaching of The Four Noble Truths, the Buddha escapes the process of rebirth. His craving is gone, he is no longer reborn, he has realized release, or *nirvana*.

The Four Noble Truths proclaim "The Middle Path" in which the body's needs are fed sufficiently for health but not indulged or starved. The First Noble Truth is that all existence, when carefully analysed, turns out to be suffering (*dukkha*). As outlined above this *dukkha* includes the physical pain involved in being born, getting sick or hurt, growing old, and dying. It also includes the frustrations that arise when pleasure turns to pain or when desires, lusts, etc., lead one to acts and mental states that cause suffering. In ordinary life we are unconscious or unaware of the suffering our daily existence entails – we are like worms in the gutter who do not know where they are. But when we become aware of our suffering and of the possibility of release, then it is as if we have only one foot in the gutter. The Second Noble Truth is that this suffering (*dukkha*) is caused by one's own acts, one's own *karma*, one's own ignorance, anger, lust, and desire. It cannot be blamed on anyone else – nature, God, one's parents, or society. The root cause of *dukkha* is one's notion of "I" or "me" and the ego-selfish desires that our sense of "I-ness" produces. The Third Noble Truth is that there is a way to end this *dukkha*, or suffering, in which we seem to be trapped. There is a way to achieve freedom from slavery to one's desires, frustrations, and anxieties. Buddha freed himself through his enlightened discovery that the "I," "Me," or "Ego" is an illusion that does not ultimately exist. When we realize that there is no permanent ego inside us, then we are freed from the selfish desires and frustrations that our illusory ego generated – desires and frustrations that caused our life to be experienced as *dukkha*. Minus ego and its selfish desiring, our life is free of *dukkha* or suffering and that is the enlightenment state realized by the Buddha – *nirvana*, consciousness in which the flame of desire has been blown out. Thus, *nirvana* is not some far-off heavenly or other-worldly state: it is simply this life in this place minus ego-selfishness. In the Buddha's experience, once ego-selfishness and the *dukkha* it causes is removed, the reality that is revealed is beautiful, harmonious, and compassionate. Just as the Buddha realized *nirvana* through his own systematic endeavor, so he has opened the path to *nirvana* for others.

The Fourth Noble Truth is really a practical path explaining how to actualize the teachings of the first three truths. After showing that our ordinary, or *samsara* experience of life is one of suffering or frustration (*dukkha*), that the cause of this suffering is desire or ego-selfishness, and that this ego-selfishness can be got rid of, Buddha goes on in the Fourth Truth to outline the means to achieve this – The Eightfold Path. "The Eightfold Path is equivalent to a shorter formula, the Threefold Training, namely morality (right speech, action and livelihood), wisdom (right views and intention) and concentration (right effort, mindfulness and concentration)."[11] Morality goes beyond mere self-mortification because it focuses on the effects of one's acts on others. Wisdom is the understanding of the teaching that results from hard study and meditation. Study of the scripture is more demanding than just the physical yogas of controlling one's breath or posture; it requires a discipline of the mind. Concentration (*samadhi*) is achieved by the cultivation of the specific skills that the Buddha learned from various teachers during his search for release. The Middle Path resulting from this Threefold Training is itself a *Yoga*, a stringent discipline that engages the whole person and causes one to turn away from the worldly life. Because the ego-selfish karmic patterns are so deeply entrenched through repeated lifetimes, the Buddha created the monasteries as places of retreat from ordinary life where monks who were serious about changing these ego-selfish patterns by following The Eightfold Path of the Buddha would be surrounded and have the support of like-minded colleagues. Within the monastery they would also have the benefit of teachers – those who were more advanced in the practice of the Eightfold Path. Buddha clearly outlined the basis for life in the monastery in his *Vinaya* – the rules for monastic life. Among other things these rules allowed for only one meal per day (today often two meals are allowed but they must be taken before noon) to be obtained from the householders of a nearby town by going door to door with one's begging bowl. *Vinaya* rules also specified no sexual activity in thought, word, or deed so as to overcome the deeply rooted karmic patterns of sexual desire built up through lifetimes of repeated sexual activity.

Since scripture records The Four Noble Truths and its initial exegesis in The Eightfold Path and the *Vinaya*, or Monastic Rules, Buddhist scripture may be said to provide the pathway from *samsara* (rebirth) to *nirvana* (release). Scripture both points to the revelation experience of the Buddha and provides a path by which others may obtain enlightenment. The Buddha, like Jesus, wrote nothing himself, and his teachings were not written down for hundreds of years. Buddhist scripture attempts to express in language the "vision" or "intuition" of reality experienced by the Buddha. Scholars differ as to what degree the scriptural descriptions can be taken as adequate verbalizations of reality or the divine. Schmithausen, for one, maintains that "In the case of Early Buddhism, most of the sources referring to Liberating Insight or Enlightenment ... do not seem to indicate that there was any problem in verbalizing experience. Therefore, these sources would seem to refer either to experiences not felt to be in conflict with concepts or to theories of Liberating Insight or Enlightenment."[12] Robinson adds that although later Buddhist (Mahayana) Doctrine elaborates the idea of the silence of the Buddha and maintains that *nirvana* is indescribable, "nowhere does the early Canon say that the content of the Enlightenment is nonintellectual, or that it is inexpressible."[13] For the early Buddhist communities (e.g. the Theravada school), Buddha's enlightenment consisted in the discovery of an experience that could be communicated via scripture, and commented upon. Yet when a seeker approached the Buddha and asked a series of questions about ultimate truth – for example, "Are the world and souls eternal, noneternal, neither or both?" – the Buddha, in some scriptures, is said to remain silent (although explaining his silence afterward to a disciple). Buddha's point would seem to have been that the language categories for existence or non-existence do not obtain at the level of *nirvana* – it is not so much a question of whether such ideas are true or false, rather, that *nirvana* transcends them.[14] Cessation of suffering (*dukkha*) is not annihilation but the overflowing of transcendence – the Buddha's experience of *nirvana* which he hinted at as being beautiful, harmonious, and compassionate.

Buddha's parable of the poisoned arrow provides a helpful illustration. A man has been struck by a poisoned arrow and a doctor has been brought to the scene. But before the man will allow the doctor to remove the arrow he wants to know: who shot the arrow; to what clan he belongs, what wood the arrow was made from; what kind of feathers were used on the arrow; and what kind of poison was on the tip. Just as the man would die before his questions were answered, said the Buddha, so also a person wishing to know the nature of his beginningless karmic ignorance and the *nirvana* experience in words will die before the Buddha would be able to describe it to him (*Majjhimaa – Nikaya Sutta*, 63).

The different schools of Buddhism, especially the major division into Theravada and Mahayana, established themselves on the basis of different commentaries written to bring out the meaning intended by the Buddha in his *Sutras*, or Sayings. All philosophical schools accept a core collection of *Sutras* and the *Vinaya*, but focus, in their commentaries, on different Sayings of the Buddha as key to the realization of salvation (*nirvana*). Let us now examine these differing systematizations of the Buddha's teaching of release.

PHILOSOPHICAL DEBATE OVER HOW TO REALIZE RELEASE (*NIRVANA*)

In the Buddha's teaching of The Four Noble Truths, several key points are highlighted. Suffering (*dukkha*) results from lack of understanding (e.g. belief in an "I" or "ego" as the true self) and the lack of self-control (e.g. allowing our emotions to run us because we do not see things as they are). The false view that feeds the emotions is that there is an eternal self (the Hindu *atman* concept) – a view which the Buddha maintained was incorrect in his teaching of the Third Noble Truth. The Buddha also significantly changed the Hindu idea of *karma-samsara*. Whereas Hinduism understood *karma* simply in terms of the action or thought itself, the Buddha emphasized the motivation behind the action as the key thing. Indeed, from the Buddha's perspective what caused one to be reborn in *dukkha* was not the memory traces of the actions or thoughts themselves, but rather the memory traces of the motivations attached to these actions or thoughts. In fact one could say that the Buddha boldly reinterpreted *karma* as motivation: "It is intention that I call *karma*," he stated.[15] This had the radical effect of shifting the doctrine of *karma* away from its categorization in terms of the actions proper to one's caste, such as one's duty to society (*dharma*) as described in the Hindu *Bhagavad Gita*, to an ethical dualism of right or wrong action as determined by one's intentions, which applied equally to all, brahmins, kings, servants, or untouchables. As Gombrich comments, "This single move overturns brahmanical, caste-bound ethics. For the intention of a brahmin cannot plausibly be claimed to be ethically of quite a different kind from the intention of an outcaste. Intention can only be virtuous or wicked."[16] The Buddha took the term "pure" as applying to the intention rather than just to the action itself. From the Buddha's perspective what makes an action good or bad is a matter of intention and choice. Actions motivated by greed, hatred, and delusion are bad while actions motivated by non-attachment, benevolence, and understanding are good. Further good actions must be pure also in doing no harm to oneself or others. Thus it is the "purely motivated" action or thought which brings the Buddhist rewards in this and future lives. And since it is the mental motivation of the action that is key, the Buddha turned the focus of *karma* to meditation – the action of purifying one's state of mind, including one's intentions. Further, such mental purification of motivations can be done directly through meditation, without any accompanying action.

Consequently, in Buddhism, morality in the world and the meditation one does in retreat are seen to be directly connected. This is reflected in the pattern the Buddha established for his monks. Two-thirds of the year they were to be out in the world teaching, healing, and solving disputes, while during the rainy season they were to withdraw into the monastery for meditation. The Buddhist prescription as to how one realizes release from rebirth (*nirvana*) is seen to require both of these activities. Good (purely motivated) deeds and a virtuous life are required but alone are not enough. Leading a moral life is only one part of the requirement for *nirvana*. The other component required is wisdom (*prajna*). Wisdom in Buddhism involves a profound philosophical understanding of the human condition, which arises only through long reflection and deep thought. As Keown puts it, "It is a kind of *gnosis*, or direct apprehension of truth which deepens over time and eventually reaches full maturity in the complete awakening experienced by the Buddha."[17] *Nirvana*, then, is realized through a fusion of pure action, or virtue, and wisdom (*prajna*). An early Buddhist text describes virtue and wisdom as two hands which wash and purify each other.[18] Buddhist ritual actions, as in the Tibetan Buddhist dalliance of the scepter with the bell in formal chanting, symbolize this same relationship. In philosophy, however, differences arise over the analysis of the human condition and the reality that makes up the wisdom (*prajna*) side of the *nirvana* equation. We will turn now to a brief overview of these philosophical differences and their impact on how to realize *nirvana*. First, we will look at the Theravada approach and second, the Mahayana.

The Theravada prescription for realizing release

The Theravada, or Early Buddhist approach is dominant in Sri Lanka and South East Asia (e.g. Thailand, Cambodia, etc.). The Theravada scholars commented on all the scriptures but focused on the Buddha's *Sutras* dealing with "No-Soul" (*anatman*), the "things" or "elements" that make up a person (*dharmas*), and the fact that all of reality is impermanent and in a state of constant change. Using these ideas of the Buddha they developed a systematic philosophical description of what composed a person. The purpose of this philosophical analysis was the therapeutic goal of convincing one that there is no permanent self, "I-ness" or "ego" inside one's personality, but that the idea of a self within is a delusion and part of the ignorance we all share in our ordinary experience. Getting rid of this delusory notion of self via the process of a philosophical analysis has the important therapeutic purpose of removing one's belief in a permanent self which, according to the Buddha's teaching of The Four Noble Truths, is the cause of the ego-selfish desiring and frustration that is turning our experience of the world into *dukkha* or suffering and preventing us from experiencing *nirvana*.

The false notion of soul, the Hindu idea of a permanently existing self or *atman*, is countered by the Buddha's teaching of *anatman* or "no-soul." A major aspect of the Buddha's enlightenment experience was the realization that everything is impermanent. This condition of impermanence applies not only to mundane things around us and our bodies, but also our sense of soul. Consequently, there is no unchanging self at the center of our human nature and therefore no basis for the notion of ego and the selfishness it produces, which turns our life into *dukkha*. We, like all other beings in the universe, are transitory and doomed to pass away in time – as we all realize when we think of ourselves as aging and finally dying. This analysis of human nature, however, gives rise to the question, "If there is no soul or self, then what is reborn?" – for Buddha did accept the Hindu idea of *samsara*, or rebirth. The Theravada analysis answers this question by developing the Buddha's teaching of the *dharmas* (elements that make up reality) into a comprehensive theory of human nature.

In response to the question "If there is no soul what is reborn?" the Theravada scholars outlined a view of human nature as composed of a series of *dharmas* or elements. These *dharmas* are the "bits and pieces," as it were, that make one up. There are *dharmas* of body, feelings, perceptions, thoughts or ideas, and consciousness that, when taken together account for our whole personality and our daily experience.[19] Just as when a mechanic takes all the bits and pieces apart that make up an automobile, there is no "car-essence" found at the center – the car is created by all the "bits and pieces" smoothly working together – similarly, when a human person is "dissected" as it were, all the *dharmas* or "bits and pieces" that make one up are laid out on the "operating table," there is no self or soul (*atman*) found at the center. The notion of a self, "I" or "ego" is a delusion created by the smooth functioning of all the parts, or *dharmas* of body, feelings, perceptions, ideas, and consciousness that make one up. The whole person is simply the sum of its parts. Nothing more, no self or ego is found or is necessary. But if these *dharmas* that make one up are impermanent, just like everything else in reality, then how can they carry forward our identity as an individual person from moment to moment, let alone from this life to the next?

To answer this question the Theravada philosophers evoke the Buddha's teaching of "dependent arising" (*pratityasamut-pada*).[20] The *dharmas* that make us up as bits of body, feeling, perception, ideas, and consciousness like all the rest of reality, are constantly changing. The idea of "dependent arising" is an explanation of how identity is maintained through this process of constant change. The arising of a *dharma* (a part that makes one up) at this moment is only possible because of its existence in a previous moment of existence. That is, its arising now is dependent on its having existed previously. And its possibility for arising as a *dharma* in a future moment is dependent on its existence in this present moment. Thus, even though each *dharma* "dies or disappears" as the present instant of time passes, its "dying" provides the occasion for the arising of a new *dharma* in the next moment in time. But this new *dharma* is as it were "in series with" and made possible by the arising and subsiding of the previous *dharmas* in the series. It is this "series connection" or "arising" that is dependent on previous "point-instants" of existence (going backwards beginning-lessly) that creates our experience of identity in the midst of constant change. The identity created by the continuity of the series of changing *dharmas* of body, feelings, etc. that make us up as persons is all that is needed to give us our sense of identity from moment to moment, day to day, or life to life. The existence of a permanent soul or self (*atman*) is shown to be unnecessary and therefore a delusion.

Once this incorrect sense of self is removed from our self-perception, the basis for ego-selfish desiring for things and experiences is also removed, and our life is no longer colored by *dukkha*. The sufferings and frustrations caused by ego-selfish desire vanish with the disappearance of the delusory notions of ego and self. And with the removal of the obstructing ignorance of a permanent self (*atman*), and the suffering and frustration it generated, the experience of *nirvana* (reality minus the desires of ego-selfishness) arises. This, from the beginning, was the therapeutic goal of the philosophical analysis of the human person by the Theravada philosophers. When the illusion of self and the flame of selfish desiring it produced was "blown out," through the twin processes of moral living and philosophical meditation on the constituent parts of human nature, the desire that pushes forward the dependent arising series of the *dharmas* disappears and the cause for rebirth is removed. A Buddhist scholar summarizes the gaining of enlightenment as follows:

> Ignorance refers to the absence of correct knowledge. An ignorant person does not know that impermanent phenomena are, in fact, impermanent. He is unable to see things as they actually are. Ignorance is not an active quality. Rather, various delusions are produced when other mental activities are influenced by ignorance ... However, just as a dream ceases as soon as a person realizes that it is a dream, so does ignorance disappear as soon as a person realizes that it is ignorance. Consequently, the purpose of the doctrine of Dependent Arising is fulfilled with the discovery of ignorance. Because ignorance is the cause of mental formations, the cessation of ignorance results in the cessation of consciousness and so on until the process results in the cessation of old age and death.[21]

The process of birth, death, and rebirth, and the constant suffering it produced, is ended and salvation, or *nirvana*, is realized.

In the Theravada tradition, a person who reached this level of *nirvana* realization is called an *arhat* (saint). An *arhat* imitates the example of the Buddha, who following his realization of enlightenment devoted the remainder of his life on earth to teaching, healing the sick, and stopping conflicts between people. In the Theravada view an *arhat* through self-effort, has purged out all impurities such as desire, hatred, ill-will, ignorance, pride, and conceit, and attained the realization of *nirvana*. An *arhat* is described as full of wisdom and compassion and after death will not be reborn.[22] From the Theravada perspective once the Buddha or an *arhat* has died they can have no more influence on those who are still living. As we will see, the Mahayana Buddhist view is quite different in this regard.

To this point I have emphasized that to become serious about reaching *nirvana*, a Buddhist should leave worldly life and join a monastery where the time and quiet needed for meditation would be provided. In the Theravada view, meditation is essential to the realization of enlightenment, and in the South Asian social environment, the peace and privacy required for meditation is generally not available. The Buddha did not consider it impossible for a layperson to attain enlightenment, and a few cases are recorded in Buddhist scriptures including the case of Buddha's own father. Tradition also suggests that should a layperson become enlightened, such a person would find it impossible to go on living in a worldly environment and would enter a monastery within the day – as Buddha's father was said to have done.[23] However, laypeople are said to have made much spiritual progress even to the point of living religious lives close to those monks or nuns, but without joining the *Sangha* or monastic order. They followed the same basic vows as those adopted by the *Sangha*, including the renouncing of sexual and economic activity. But the Buddha's general expectation was that the role of those in the householder stage of life was to provide food and economic support to the monks and nuns, and to follow a less stringent practice than was required for the attainment of salvation. Laypeople were to observe five precepts: abstention from killing, stealing, sexual misconduct, false speech, and intoxicants.[24] Nor, in traditional Theravada society, did laypeople have full access to all of the Buddha's teachings. In general the Buddha's view seems to have been that the full teaching was reserved for those who were seriously enough interested in attaining salvation that they would give up the householder life to become monks or nuns. Only then would they have the time, privacy, quiet, and support needed for serious meditation on the key teachings.

The rules and organization for the *Sangha* were given by the Buddha in his *Vinaya* teaching. Persons over twenty years old could receive full ordination and become monks or nuns. Those below the age of twenty could be initiated and enter the *Sangha* as male or female novices, with a usual minimum age of fourteen, lowered in special cases to seven. Of the approximately 250 rules in the *Vinaya* the most important (four for monks, eight for nuns) deal with abstention from sexual intercourse, stealing, taking human life, and lying about one's spiritual achievements. Commission of any of these acts meant lifelong expulsion from the order. Next in importance came a second set of thirteen rules for monks and seventeen for nuns dealing with such things as sexual offenses, false accusations against another monk or nun, and attempts to cause schisms in the order. If a person commits any of these acts, he or she is required to go before a meeting of the *Sangha* and confess his or her wrongdoings. Then for seven days the sinner must live apart from the order and do penance. Then the order may meet and readmit the person if they are satisfied with his or her penance. A third set of rules dealt with offenses of undetermined seriousness (with the seriousness determined by the evidence given by witnesses) of monks found with women. A fourth set gives thirty rules for monks and nuns relating to such matters as possession of robes (only three are allowed), begging bowls, gold, silver, jewelry, and medicine. If these rules are violated, the items in question must be surrendered and the person confess his or her wrongdoing. A fifth set of rules, numbering about ninety-two for monks and two hundred for nuns, concern minor offenses such as speaking harshly or lying and require confession. Three other sets of rules deal with acceptance of inappropriate food, procedures for begging, eating, and preaching, and finally rules for the resolution of disputes within the order.[25]

Life within the monastery was designed to help monks and nuns curb their desires and thus make progress toward *nirvana*. A typical day would involve rising early and meditating. Later in the morning one would go out to beg for one's food and then return to eat with the other monks or nuns before noon (only one meal a day is generally allowed and nothing is to be eaten after noon hour). In the afternoon one could visit the homes of lay believers or go to the forest to meditate. In the evening group discussions focusing on the Buddha's teachings might be held in the monastery or one might have a meeting with one's teacher. Finally one would withdraw to one's own room for more meditation and go to sleep late at night. Six times each month laypeople come to the monastery and the monks preach the teachings of the Buddha to them. Twice each month the monks or nuns gather to do this for themselves and to chant together the rules for monastic life established by the Buddha – the *pratimoksa*. If this seems a very austere and ascetic monastic practice, one should remember that from Buddha's perspective this was a "middle way" between the extreme of rigorous asceticism, such as was practiced by the Jaina monks of his day, and the luxuries of worldly life. It was a path that would simply sustain bodily life in such a way that the time and support for the virtuous living and meditational practice needed for the realization of *nirvana* were provided to the serious searcher.

A major change in Theravada practice was initiated in nineteenth-century Ceylon – a change that Gombrich has named "Protestant Buddhism."[26] British missionaries brought the printing press to Ceylon and engaged Buddhist monks to help them translate and print the Christian scriptures. Some monks copied this idea and set up their own printing presses. They began by publishing pamphlets countering the attacks of the Protestant Christian missionaries on Buddhism. But soon the monks moved on to the printing and distribution of Buddhist texts themselves. This opened up to Buddhist laypeople the knowledge that up until then had been maintained by oral transmission within the monastery, and had been the restricted special knowledge of the monks. At the same time the Buddhist laity were taking the lead in establishing village schools to compete with those being set up by the Christian missionaries. In 1869 the first non-monastic Buddhist school was organized in Ceylon. These schools and the new printing presses combined to produce a lay reading public for the first time in Buddhist circles in Ceylon. In addition, following the model of British Protestant Colleges, Buddhist Colleges were established admitting both monks and laity into Buddhist Studies programs. This "Protestantization" of Buddhism was further aided and abetted by the arrival of Colonel Olcott and the Theosophical Society in Ceylon in 1875. Olcott formally embraced Buddhism, taking the Three Refuges and Five Precepts. As a colonel and a judge, Olcott had a high profile. He was also an experienced organizer and united the different factions among Sinhalese Buddhism. In 1881 he published in English his *Buddhist Catechism*, a summary of the basic teachings to which he felt all the Buddhists in the world should be able to subscribe. Various versions of this *Catechism* have been used in the lay Buddhist movements in Ceylon which have fostered the teaching of Buddhism outside the monasteries. These organizations modeled themselves on Protestant Christian institutions (e.g. the Young Men's Buddhist Association, modeled after the Y.M.C.A.). The Y.M.B.A. set up a national network of Buddhist Sunday Schools and commissioned, printed, and distributed the Buddhist texts for them until these functions were taken over in the 1960s by the government.[27]

In the late 1800s in Ceylon a person arose who became a national hero for the "Protestant Buddhist" movement. Anagarika Dharmapala was born to a middle class family, educated in Anglican schools, but was taught and practiced Buddhism at home with his mother. He met Colonel Olcott in 1880, acted as his interpreter, and worked for the Theosophical Society until 1898 when they parted company. In 1891 Dharmapala visited Bodh Gaya, in Northern India – the place where the Buddha attained his enlightenment. Bodh Gaya was then in a derelict state and under Hindu control. Dharmapala established the Maha Bodhi Society to win back for Buddhists ownership of Bodh Gaya. This was accomplished after his death and today Bodh Gaya is an important pilgrimage site for Buddhists worldwide. Regarding Ceylon, Dharmapala introduced two important innovations. He introduced a nationalist thrust into Buddhism in Ceylon, and he gave the layperson a new status that went well beyond organizational leadership. Traditionally lay Buddhists did not meditate – that was reserved for the monks in their pursuit of *nirvana*. But in 1890 Dharmapala found an old text on meditation which he himself studied and had published. He thus became the first Buddhist to learn meditation from a book – a practice which he then commended to the Buddhist laity.[28]

In his appropriation of the Protestant ethos into Theravada Buddhism in Ceylon, Dharmapala created a new status halfway between a monk and a layperson. Instead of the monk's yellow robe he wore a white robe. He did not shave his head but he adopted a life of chastity and ascetic practice. He publicly committed his life to Buddhism, but without renouncing worldly activity. Dharmapala accepted the Christian criticism of monks as selfish. His revision of Buddhism was directed not just to seeking his own salvation (the approach of the monasteries as he saw them) but for the general welfare of Buddhists worldwide. In Dharmapala's view the Buddha's teaching of salvation was open to laypeople, who could read his teachings and meditate, as well as to monks and nuns. This "Protestant Buddhist" approach continues to be practiced by the urbanized middle class, largely English-educated, in Sri Lanka today. Gombrich concludes that the major contribution of "Protestant Buddhism", namely, its emphasis on lay religiosity, is alive and well. "The layman should permeate his life with his Buddhism; this means both that he should himself strive for *nirvana*, without necessarily entering the *Sangha* to do so, and that he should do what he can to make

Buddhism permeate society."[29] Meditation and the study of all the Buddha's teachings (traditionally activities reserved for monks and nuns) are now available to laypeople, male and female, young and old, in their search for salvation.

The Mahayana prescription for realizing release

The Mahayana approach to salvation develops in conflict with the interpretation of the Buddha's teaching by the Theravada, or Tradition of the elders. The evolution of the Mahayana began after the time of Buddha's death, continued through the Second Council during Asoka's reign, and was almost complete by the first century B.C.E.[30] Mahayana scholars in their commentaries focus on such passages in the *Sutras* as the silence of the Buddha in response to questions of a metaphysical nature (e.g. Is the world eternal or not? Will the Buddha exist after death or not? Is the soul or self identical to or different from the body?) or the Buddha's parable of the wounded man who wanted to know all about the poisoned arrow stuck in his chest before he would allow it to be removed. Early on the advocates of Mahayana teachings were few in number and were branded as heretics and breakers of the Orthodox Order of the Elders (the Theravada). However, by about the beginning of the Common Era the Mahayana had become dominant, spreading from Northern India to China, and later to Tibet and Japan.[31] Major points of difference (or "heresy" from a Theravada perspective) included a desire to extend the Buddhist Canon of scripture to include new *Sutras*, or sayings of the Buddha, a change in understanding of the nature of the Buddha himself, and the attributing of imperfections to the *Arhats*.[32]

The *Arhats*, the enlightened saints who have realized *nirvana*, are described by one Mahadeva as open to ignorance, seduction, doubt, etc. Parallel to this lowering of the *Arhat*'s status is a raising of the status of the Buddha to something more than just a purely human being. Although he was born in this world, he was, it is suggested, not tainted by it. The popular literature that grew up after the Buddha's death recounts his many virtuous deeds in previous lives as a *Bodhisattva*, or one on the path to Buddhahood. Because of the merit the Buddha built up in previous lives, his birth and life take on supra-human qualities: he is conceived without sexual intercourse; he emerges from his mother's right side without pain; and, as the text of the *Mahavatsu* puts it, he merely appears to wash, eat, sit in the shade, take medicine, etc., out of conformity to the ways of the world.[33] The Buddha is said to be omniscient, never to sleep but to be always in meditation. This finally leads to the teaching of some Mahayana scholars that the Buddha's death was also a mere appearance – in reality he remains present in this world out of compassion, helping suffering humanity. Following this new image of the Buddha, the salvation goal for humans to strive toward is not to become an *Arhat* but to take the *Bodhisattva* vow (not to go into *nirvana* until all other beings have realized release) and "embark on the long path to a supreme, totally superior Buddhahood."[34]

The claim of the continued presence of the Buddha after his death allowed Mahayana monks to associate the Buddha's name with *Sutras* composed after his death – and therefore outside the closed canon of the earthly utterances of the Buddha held to by the Theravada tradition. Thus around the first century B.C.E. the above developments resulted in the appearance of a new literature, the *Mahayana Sutras*, which claim to be the word of the Buddha himself, composed in his lifetime but concealed until later. Not the product of a single group or movement, these new *Sutras* arose from different groups of monks, nuns and, sometimes laypersons practicing within existing Buddhist traditions. These *Sutras* focus on the supremacy of the Buddha, the path of the *Bodhisattva*, and concern for the well-being of all. These monks, nuns, and perhaps a small number of householders who accepted this new literature formed a series of cults probably based on the different *Sutras*. Some "may have felt themselves in direct contact with a Buddha who inspired them in meditation or in dreams. Sometimes they proclaimed the Doctrine itself, embodied in the text, as the body of the Buddha,"[35] his ever-present "Dharma-body," which was judged much superior to the relics of the historical Buddha (e.g. a tooth) that had been placed in *stupas*, or burial mounds, and used as a focus for Theravada worship. Although a minority within Indian Buddhism, their numbers increased as time passed until they identified their approach to salvation as a *Mahayana*, or superior way.

According to Williams the key characteristic of the *Mahayana Sutras* is that "the *Sutra* is not one object among others, but rather is the body of the Buddha, a focus of celebration and worship on the model of relic worship."[36] As such the *Mahayana Sutras* are sacred books that are not only memorized by repeated chanting, copied, and studied, but are also themselves objects of worship. Each monk or nun probably owned no more than one or two *Sutras* which would be rapidly learned by heart through repeated chanting and through use as a focus for meditation. These texts were used as a basis for exposition by teachers in terms of their own experience and their lineage of previous teachers traced back to the Buddha himself. In this way the *Mahayana Sutras,* or sacred texts, provided a basis for teaching, study, meditation, and worship by which one could realize *nirvana*. The sacred texts still function this way in traditional Mahayana cultures such as Tibetan Buddhism, where the *Sutras* also serve as the basis for the sacred art of the tradition.

The *Mahayana Sutras* vary in length from a few words to over 100,000 verses in the longest *Perfection of Wisdom sutra*, with the longer ones likely having grown and developed over the centuries in different countries (e.g. China). The earliest

Mahayana Sutras seem to be the *Prajnaparamita Sutras*, which probably originated in central or southern India and became quite influential in northwest India during the first century C.E. Conze has distinguished four phases in the development of the *Prajnaparamita* literature, beginning about 100 B.C.E. and stretching over one thousand years.[37] These texts seem to provide the foundations for much Mahayana philosophical thought. The concept of *prajna* (wisdom) and its perfection developed in these texts, refers to a combination of conceptual and non-conceptual understanding gained through meditation, such as the non-conceptual and direct awareness of *sunya* (the universal absence of any ultimate existence as the true characteristic of all *dharmas*). Ultimate *prajna*, as understood by Mahayana and the *Prajnaparamita Sutra*, refers to a number of perfections to be mastered by the *Bodhisattva* as he or she follows the long path to perfect Buddhahood, including giving (*dana*), morality (*sila*), patience (*ksanti*), effort (*virya*), meditative concentration (*dhyana*), and wisdom (*prajna*). Wisdom (*prajna*) is often given the primary emphasis, and within that the extension of the Buddha's teaching of no-self to equal no-essence is key. The central critique is of the Theravada claim to have found some things that really ultimately exist, i.e. *dharmas*. The radical Mahayana critique meant that anyone attempting to practice these teachings in meditation had to engage in a complete "letting go" of all conceptual belief and discursive analysis – a giving up of all intellectual attachment which could be achieved, according to Williams, only as the truth of emptiness was realized.[38] This teaching, as basic to the practice of the *Bodhisattva* in the perfection of *nirvana*, provided ample grounds for a different philosophical interpretation to develop.

The great Indian philosopher Nagarjuna (second century C.E.) is taken to be the founder of the Madhyamaka school (within the Mahayana tradition) with his great work the *Mulamadhyamakakarika*. In it Nagarjuna develops a critique of the Theravada theory of *dharmas* as the elements or parts that make up the whole person. Basing himself on the silence of the Buddha in response to the unanswerable questions such as "Does the self or soul exist after death or not?", Nagarjuna criticized the Theravada philosophers' confidence that we could conceptually know things just as they are. This approach, as we saw above, was to analyze phenomena (e.g. a person) for the *dharmas* or essences (*svabhava*) that made them up. Such an analysis, said the Theravadas, resulted in an absolutely true view of things, which they termed ultimate truth (*paramartha-satya*), in contrast to the relative, commonsense beliefs of the less insightful, which were termed relative truth or worldly convention (*samvrtisatya*).[39] The aim was to come to understand and accept the correct view and then through meditation one could actualize its meaning in one's daily life. Through this "philosophical therapy" the Theravada path aimed at a final awakening (*nirvana*) through a step-by-step process of understanding, meditation, and practice. The difficulty with this from Nagarjuna's critical perspective was that the Theravada approach put conceptual knowledge at the center. Unless one had an ultimately true view of things (*paramarthasatya*), one could not hope to follow a meditation that would lead to release. Nagarjuna deconstructed this Theravada approach. In reaction to the Hindu *atman* (self is ultimately real), the Theravada Buddhists had made the mistake of swinging the pendulum to the opposite extreme and adopting a *dharma* view, according to which the parts that make up the person are ultimately real. Like the silence of the Buddha, Nagarjuna's aim is to show the hollowness of all viewpoints and put an end to all attempts to conceptualize reality through language, leaving only silent meditation as the path to release.

Nagarjuna's critique rests on the perceived discontinuity between the way the world is and what philosophy thinks the world to be. Suspicious of any absolute claim made about the nature of reality (such as the Hindu and Theravada claims),

Nagarjuna shows "that the philosopher engaged in such metaphysics is living a sick form of life, infecting others who take him seriously."[40] The only cure for this disease is to demonstrate the utter hollowness of all metaphysical claims through the deconstructive analysis offered by *reductio ad absurdum* argument. Nagarjuna develops this approach in his *Mulamadhyamakarika*.[41] Nagarjuna's four-pronged negation shows the futility of attempting to take any sort of ultimate philosophical position. Conceptual language is useful for everyday purposes such as buying a loaf of bread, but when it is used to make ultimate claims it becomes deceptive and entrapping: saying "x exists" becomes the basis for the belief that "x actually exists." Psychologically, one has fallen into the trap of becoming ego-attached to one's own philosophical or theological worldview. This is not simply a case of falling in love with the theory we have created or adopted, it also plays the role of providing for us a shelter from the anxiety and insecurity faced by the ego when the partiality and ultimate emptiness of all worldviews is realized. But Nagarjuna's aim is not nihilism and the psychological depression it might induce. Rather it is the freeing of one from seeing everyday reality through "philosophical or theological glasses" that give only a partial and distorted perception. Nagarjuna's *catuskoti* technique is a method for deconstructing our distorting "philosophical or theological glasses" so that reality is no longer experienced through the subject-object and subject-predicate filtering of language. Once this enlightened state is realized, the application of the *catuskoti* is no longer necessary – the philosophical disease has been overcome and the patient is cured.[42] The need, both psychological and epistemological (for a worldview we can put our trust in as absolute truth), has been totally overcome. Reality is immediately experienced just as it is, and that is *nirvana* – this world minus ego-selfish desiring and philosophizing. Thus Nagarjuna's famous dictum "*samsara is nirvana*." *Nirvana* is not the end of rebirth as the Hindus and Theravadas taught, but a rebirth in which each life is lived in compassion for others, without trace of ego-selfish desires or the distorting worldviews that turn life into *dukkha* or suffering.

Madhyamaka Buddhism sees language, with its construction of the forms of subject and object, as ontologically empty – as unable to encapsulate the truth of ultimate reality as the Buddha's silence signified.[43] Rather than making us self-aware, these imaginary constructions act as obstacles to the clear perception of reality. Thus the need for the negation of the structures of language for the spiritual realization of salvation to proceed. Even the oral and written scriptures of Buddhism must eventually be transcended if *nirvana* is to be realized. Seen from an ultimate (*paramartha*) perspective, all words, even those of the Buddha, are empty (*sunya*) of reality.[44] The goal of Nagarjuna's deconstructive critique of language (his *catuskoti*) is not to reduce the holders of a philosophical or theological viewpoint (*drsti*) to nihilism, but to sensitize them to the interdependent (*pratitya-samutpada*) universe of which they are merely a part, and to act in conformity to its inherent compassion – which the Buddha's enlightenment has revealed. For Nagarjuna the subject-object separation, that language necessarily seems to create, prevents one from reaching the spiritual goal while under its sway. As long as one approaches reality through the viewpoints or *drstis* of language, *pratitya-samutpada* and one's necessary place within it will never be seen. Thus the necessity to go beyond language through the silence of meditation into direct experience in which no subject-object duality is present. For Nagarjuna, language, even the sacred words of scripture, does not seem able to participate in the final spiritual goal.

But this very negative critique of language as a means to salvation seems tempered by some Mahayana scholars and traditions (e.g. Zen). A contemporary Mahayana scholar, David Loy, offers a more positive assessment of the role of language in salvation and cites Nagarjuna in support. Loy points out that the assumption that a distinction can be made between an "apparent world" mediated by language and the "real world" unmediated by language is inconsistent with the fundamental tenet of Nagarjuna that "*samsara* is *nirvana*" (language being very much part of *samsara*). *Sunyata*, says Loy referencing *Mulamadhyamakarika* XIII:7–8 and XXII:11, is intended by Nagarjuna to be a therapy to get one to release, not an ultimate truth or an ontological category. "In other words, emptiness, the relativity of all things, is itself relative; the ultimate truth, like the conventional, is devoid of independent being."[45] The end of views such as "ultimate" and "conventional" leaves the world as it really is – a *sunyata* or non-dual world in which there is no philosophical or theological meddling but in which language still participates. We speak, just as we act; but we do not cling to any action or conceptual system. "If there is no subject-object separation between language and object, between signifier and signified, then all phenomena, including words, are *tatha*, 'thusness.' That is why, as we clearly see in the Zen tradition, language too participates in the reality it manifests ... [otherwise] how could so many Zen dialogues have led to a realization on the part of the student."[46] This makes clear Loy's different interpretation of Nagarjuna as ending in a spiritual realization that is in one sense beyond language, but in which language still participates – as we see in Zen *koan* practice and some Tibetan or Japanese Jodo-Shinsu *mantra* chanting.

The above is only a brief and incomplete outline of Nagarjuna's teaching with regard to release. A more complete summary can be found in Paul Williams, *Mahayana Buddhism*, along with references to other Madhyamaka scholars we have not mentioned. Williams also offers a good treatment of the Yogacara or "Mind Only" school that develops as a response to Nagarjuna and the Madhyamaka school – along with other Mahayana developments such as the *Tathagatagarbha*

(Buddha-essence/Buddha-nature), the Chinese *Hua-yen* (Flower Garland tradition), the *Lotus Sutra*, and Tibetan Tantric Buddhism.[47] While these developments were important to the philosophically minded *nirvana* seekers, the larger number of Mahayana followers sought salvation through religious practices based on the *Bodhisattva* path. During the early centuries the *Bodhisattva* model was worked out in some detail beginning with the appearance of a strong motivation to become a *Bodhisattva* in order to save others – the "thought of enlightenment" or *Bodhicitta* experience. The person then seeks initiation as a *Bodhisattva* and takes a vow to save all beings by leading them to *nirvana* no matter how long it takes. The aspiring *Bodhisattva* practices the six Mahayana virtues mentioned earlier (generosity, morality, patience, courage, meditation, and wisdom) and progresses through a system of ten *bhumis* or stages. On reaching the seventh stage it is held to be certain that one will reach *nirvana*, and that it is impossible to fall back.

Bodhisattvas who had reached the higher stages were visualized as very powerful and virtually equivalent to the Buddha in his ever-present or heavenly form. One who has attained such a high status is Avalokitesvara (the Lord who looks down in compassion) of whom the Tibetan Dalai Lamas are said to be incarnations. Avalokitesvara is depicted with many arms reaching out to help those who are suffering. In East Asia he changed sex and became Kwan-yin in China, Kannon in Japan. Manjusri, another such *Bodhisattva* of high attainment, carries the flaming sword of wisdom which cuts through ignorance. Over the centuries a vast pantheon of Buddhas and *Bodhisattvas* "is conceived of as inhabiting a majestic unseen universe. Just as our own world system was graced by a Buddha, it seemed not unreasonable to suppose that others had been too. The Mahayana therefore proceeded to invent names and characteristics for these fictional Buddhas and located them in magnificent Buddha-realms."[48] A common depiction shows a group of five Buddhas in a circular pattern called a *mandala*. These *mandalas* can be focused upon, painted, or drawn in the sand as forms of meditation. A typical arrangement places the historical Buddha at the center with four celestial Buddhas seated around him: Amitabha ("Infinite Light") to the west; Absobhya ("the Imperturbable") to the east; Ratnasambhava ("the Jewel Born" representing Buddha as giver of gifts) to the south; and Amoghasiddhi ("Infinite Success," Buddha's miraculous power to save) to the north. Some depictions show various *Bodhisattvas* seated on petals in between.[49] Amitabha, the western Buddha, became the focus of a popular East Asian cult which formed around the idea of a "Pure Land" he was thought to inhabit. Amitabha (Amida in Japan) took a vow that he would help anyone who called upon him with true faith to ensure that they would be reborn in his Pure Land (*Sukhavati*). In contrast to the Theravada tradition where the most the Buddha offered was his teaching and personal example and it was up to the person to make their own effort to follow, here we find in Mahayana practice the suggestion that salvation in the form of rebirth in the Pure Land can be attained through faith in Amitabha and the grace he will give. But even in this tradition some individual effort is still required, for the Pure Land or western paradise of Amitabha is not the same as *nirvana*. A person reborn there would still need to make a final effort to gain full enlightenment. In fact the geographical and artistic representations of the Pure Land as a magnificent western paradise may use notions of faith and grace to begin with but are designed to eventually give one the insight that "If there are mountains in this world, and all is flat in the Pure Land, that is because there are mountains in the mind." This impure world is indeed the Pure Land. It only appears impure because of the impurities in our minds. "Thus the real way to attain a Pure Land is to purify one's own mind. Put another way, we are already in the Pure Land if we but knew it ... The Pure Land is truly, therefore, not a 'heavenly abode' but enlightenment itself."[50] This is the result of the final self-effort that has to be made. In the Japanese Jodo Shinshu tradition, it is the "far end" of the simple congregational and individual chanting of the *nembutsu* (*Namu Amida Butsu*, "I surrender myself to Amida Buddha") that the most simple layperson can do.[51] The Jodo Shinshu tradition, which with its clergy, laity, and congregational worship looks thoroughly "protestantized," offers a devotional practice for purifying the mind that the most lowly layperson can follow and yet, with sufficient sincerity of surrender, reach Nagarjuna's realization that "*samsara* is *nirvana*" – one's own impure mind of this world, when purified, is the Pure Land of *nirvana*. As Williams notes this is only "a short step from the Chan (Zen) notion that the Pure Land is the tranquil, clear, radiant, pure Mind,"[52] but in this Zen case a realization to be reached by rigorous meditation on the flow of one's breath (*zazen*). In this great variety of ways Mahayana Buddhism offers paths to salvation (*nirvana*) that serve monks, nuns, and laypeople alike.

7

Conclusion

The chapters of this book offer a brief introduction to the understandings of sin and salvation found within the major world religions. By way of conclusion let us briefly review the findings of the preceding chapters.

Rather than "salvation," Judaism speaks of "redemption" for individuals, for Israel and for all the nations. God is understood as the creator, revealer, and redeemer. God rescued Israel from bondage in Egypt in the past, redeems faithful people in their everyday lives, and in the Torah promises redemption in the future. As humans we are trapped between what Torah or scripture tells us to do and what we are able to achieve. What the Torah required from people was not just religious observance but also moral behaviour. As the great prophets, such as Jeremiah made clear, God is active in history, in daily life and calls people, through Torah to work with God in doing away with poverty and injustice. In spite of people's deceitful and stubborn ways, the Torah presents a vision of how human failure will be overcome on "the day of the Lord" that the Messiah will usher in in the future. In the meantime humans struggle with their tendencies toward both good and evil in a world where evil constantly threatens the soul with death. For Jews of the modern period, this is especially true as they try to cope with the evil of the Holocaust and yet still maintain their faith in God and their hope for ultimate redemption.

In the chapter on Judaism we saw how the Sages or teachers of the oral Law interpret the image of a Messiah to be a bringer of righteousness into the world (e.g. Is. 11:1–10) rather than that of a saviour as in Christianity. In Judaism redemption is dependent on the repentance and good deeds of the people of Israel which, according to some, will also bring the redemption of the whole world. This scriptural idea of redemption went through many stages of evolution as a result of experiences such as the Babylonian exile, loss of the Temple in Jerusalem, and, in the last century, the Holocaust. We traced this evolution from the earliest scriptures of the Torah, the Pentateuch, through the prophets, the Sages of the Oral Torah, medieval philosophy, and the mystics of the Kabbalah to modern thinkers such as Buber, Heschel, and Rosenzweig. Martin Buber, for example, sees redemption as the eradication of human-caused evil in history through the sanctifying of daily life – by turning away from evil and toward God in our everyday activities. God helps us to do this by reaching out to us through grace. In the final section of the chapter we traced the Jewish thinking of life after death from the early idea that there is no survival beyond the grave (immortality comes through one's children) to the later conception of a bodily resurrection. Notions of a bodily resurrection, a Messiah, and judgement in an afterlife, became engaged in discussions of redemption. In modern Jewish thought, Orthodox Judaism has continued to understand redemption in terms of physical resurrection and an afterlife, whereas for many non-Orthodox Jews ideas of an afterlife are virtually absent and redemption is conceived almost entirely as a religious dimension of this life.

Christianity offers perhaps the clearest example of a salvation religion. Christianity began when Jesus preached about God saying "Repent and believe in the good news" (Mk.

1:14). According to Christian thinking the incarnation and death of Jesus Christ formed the climax of God's plan for the salvation of people. This plan became necessary after Adam, the forefather of the human race, fell from grace into sin and death as a result of his disobedience. God's plan to save humans from Adam's fate will be completed at the time of the Last Judgement when the second coming of Christ will mark the end of the world. We saw many echoes of Jewish ideas of redemption in Christian thought, along with some key differences. The notion of a Messiah, as envisioned by the Hebrew prophets like Isaiah, is taken over by Christians with Jesus Christ being identified as the Messiah. The idea of a bodily resurrection of the dead is also absorbed with the resurrection of Jesus from the tomb as the first example. Unlike some Jewish ideas, however, the raising of people from their graves for final judgement does not take place with the arrival of Jesus, the Messiah, but awaits his second coming, following his death and resurrection. As was the case in Judaism the saving activity of God engages the whole world including both people and nature and thus is thought of as the salvation history of the cosmos. Unlike Judaism, Christianity suggests that Adam's disobedience to God in the garden of Eden is inherited by all humans (and nature) as original sin and death. But there is considerable agreement with Jewish ideas of an afterlife in which death will be overcome and a day of judgement will take place with appropriate rewards or punishments in Heaven or Hell.

Christian ideas regarding sin and salvation evolved from the New Testament thinking of the early followers of Jesus through the Christian Fathers such as Origen to Augustine, Aquinas, and the reformers Luther and Calvin. Protestant teaching broke the identification of sin and salvation with the Church by its teaching of the "priesthood of all believers," – the idea that all believers can relate directly to God, without the mediation of priests and the sacraments of the Church. The idea of "the priesthood of all believers" meant that all Christians are to be embodiments of God's saving word, and that no single church could monopolize the mediation of God's grace since there were believers in all churches, Roman Catholic, Orthodox, and Protestant. As opposed to the medieval emphasis on theology (e.g. Augustine and Aquinas) or on the Church's sacraments for salvation, Protestants rediscovered the Bible and its teachings as the primary impetus for saving faith. For followers of the Eastern Orthodox Christian Church salvation is understood not in terms of Christ paying a debt for the sin of Adam – as in the West – but as uniting the human and the divine through the power of the Holy Spirit, with the divine overcoming human sin and, finally, exalting humans to divine life. Contemporary Christians, as we saw, struggle with how to adapt the biblical and early Christian views of sin, salvation, death, and afterlife to the modern world. Science has made it impossible to hang on to ideas of Heaven and Hell in a three-storey universe. So some Christians think of Heaven and Hell as descriptions of the way we live our lives here and now – as the Kingdom of God on earth. Christian feminist scholars, like Sallie McFague, argue that salvation must be brought down to earth and include the health and well-being of earth, air, water, plants, and animals along with humans. In this view responsibility for the salvation of creation is ours not God's. By our everyday choices we participate in either the destruction of creation, or its salvation.

The chapter on Islam reviewed several Qur'anic terms with salvation-like qualities. *Najat*, translated as "salvation" means escaping the punishment of the fires of Hell. In the Qur'an Muhammad teaches that obedience and submission to Allah is the way to salvation, for Allah is merciful. Unlike Christianity's idea of salvation as redemption from sin, in Islam salvation is conceived as escape from the fires of Hell by following God's guidance (*huda*). Following God's guidance in the Qur'an brings one out of darkness and into the light, out of polytheism and into worship of the one God, out of lawlessness and into loving obedience, which at the Day of Judgement will land one in Heaven rather than Hell. This Qur'anic guidance leads to *falah*, prosperity and success in this world and the next. Salvation depends on human effort as well as God's mercy in following the Qur'an's teachings.

According to Islam humans are created with the freedom to choose but also with the obligation to observe God's law revealed in the Qur'an, and in so doing to help bring about moral order in human history. By doing good and rejecting evil as taught in the Qur'an, humans evolve morally and spiritually until salvation is realized. Here the presence of the *Umma*, the Muslim community, is essential for the nurturing of the individual toward salvation. The chapter on Islam reviews various views as to how one is to escape the fires of Hell's torment to the rewards of Paradise, including salvation by the will of Allah, salvation by the mercy of Allah, salvation as the reward of faith, salvation through faith and works combined, salvation through intercession by the prophets, and salvation via the Sufi mystical path. Here the considerable differences within the Sunni, Shi'ite and Sufi approaches were observed. Regarding salvation and the afterlife the Muslim view is presented in very graphic detail. Shortly after burial the deceased is visited by two angels and is made to answer questions of the faith. If one answers correctly one is left alone until the resurrection of the dead and the Day of Judgement. If not the person is struck on the face and the back as a foretaste of the punishment to follow. On the day of resurrection all the dead are brought back to life to stand before God to answer for their actions, which are read out and weighed in the scales of divine judgement. Those who pass prosper in Paradise while those who do not are consigned to the fires of Hell. Some passages of the Qur'an allow for intercession by the prophets, especially Muhammad, on behalf of believers. Vivid descriptions are offered of both Paradise and Hell. Ordinary Muslims feel the issue of sin and salvation strongly. Rather than debating about it, they devote themselves to actions they know will please God, realizing that the final decision about their afterlife is in God's hands.

In the last two chapters our focus shifted to the religions of Asia, Hinduism and Buddhism. There sin or disobedience to God is replaced by ignorance as the basic human condition from which we wish to be saved. Rather than salvation or redemption from sin with the help of God's grace, release from repeated rebirth is the spiritual goal – usually envisaged as enlightenment that extinguishes the ignorance that is causing us to be reborn. Both Hinduism and Buddhism share the idea of four stages of life: student, householder, forest dweller and holy wanderer. These four *asramas*, as they are called, provide a framework for the religious, psychological, and social needs of the individual from childhood to old age. As we saw in Hinduism (chapter 5) this idea of stages of life along with the veil of karmic ignorance is what hides from us the truth of our divine natures and the salvation or release that would bring. We noted that a great strength of Hinduism was its understanding that God, through the Vedas or Hindu scriptures, provides several paths to release, leaving it to the devotee to select the path (*Marga*) which best suits his or her disposition. Four paths to *moksa*, or release, were discussed: knowledge (*Jnana Marga*), action (*Karma Marga*), devotion (*Bhakti Marga*), and self-discipline (*Yoga Marga*). These paths were given systematic development by major thinkers who composed commentaries based on seed ideas found in scriptures such as the *Upanisads* or the *Bhagavad Gita*. Such commentaries often established schools of thought and spiritual practices that have continued to evolve in the living traditions of Hinduism right up to the present. We followed Sankara's knowledge (*jnana*) path of release from its inception *c.* 800 C.E. up to its recent exponents, Vivekananda and Ramana Maharshi. By contrast Ramanuja (*c.* 1050 C.E.) systematized a devotional (*bhakti*) approach based on the *Bhagavad Gita* and the Tamil poet saints, the *alvars*. This path, adopted by the Hindu masses, was brought to North America by Swami Bhaktivedanta in the 1960s as the International Society for Krishna Consciousness (I.S.K.C.O.N.). The path of action (*karma*) also takes its rise from the *Bhagavad Gita* and has been championed in recent times by Mahatma Gandhi. The *Yoga* path, as we saw, was systematized by Patanjali (*c.* 200 C.E.) in his *Yoga Sutras*, with new commentaries on his work still being written today. The thought of a contemporary exponent of *Yoga*, Sri Aurobindo, was briefly examined.

The above four paths to release were found to represent the dominant Hindu thinking on salvation and how to reach it. Unlike Judaism, Christianity, and Islam little attention is given to the afterlife since in the Hindu view the afterlife is nothing more than being reborn on earth over and over again until, through the practice of one of the paths, the obscuring ignorance (*karma*) is burnt off and release (*moksa*) is realized. This is salvation and it will occur during a life on earth after which one will not be reborn but will enjoy eternal union or communion with the divine.

Buddhists, as we saw in chapter 6, share much with Hindus in their analysis of the human condition from which we seek to be saved. As for Hindus the basic problem is one of ignorance, but the Buddha (*c.* 500 B.C.E.) did not find the Hindu answer as to how to find release from rebirth satisfactory. In his analysis of the ignorance that is holding us back, the Buddha discovered that its cause is our belief that within us there is an "I," "ego," or "self" that is unchanging. In his enlightenment experience the Buddha discovered that the notion of an "I" or "self" within is illusory. It is this false notion of a permanent self or soul within that causes us to experience life as suffering (*dukkha*) and to be reborn. Release results from the realization that there is no ego, soul, or self within and thus nothing to cause the selfish desiring. *Nirvana* is this ordinary everyday world minus ego-selfishness. As to how to reach this state of release, the Buddha was quite clear that there is no God that will save us, rather it is a realization that must be won by each of us through our own effort. What the Buddha did do was to leave his own insight and teaching as an example that we can adopt on the basis of provisional trust and try out for ourselves. But only if it proves out in our own experience should we accept it as a way to release. This teaching was formulated by the Buddha as The Four Noble Truths, including The Eightfold Path to release or enlightenment, and became the scripture of Buddhism.

For those who are serious about undertaking the path to release (*nirvana*) the Buddha established the monastery and the *Vinaya*, or rules by which the monks and nuns are to live. After Buddha's death philosophical debates arose among his followers over the interpretation of his teachings. The Theravada school focused on the Buddha's sayings dealing with "No-Soul" (*anatman*), the things or elements (*dharmas*) that make us up, and the fact that all of reality is impermanent and in a state of constant change. Using these ideas they developed a philosophical analysis of what composed a person, showing that since there is no permanent self or ego within there is no basis for desiring possessions or sensuous experiences that turn our lives into *dukkha* (suffering, frustration), thus opening the door to the realization of *nirvana*. In the Theravada tradition, a person who has reached this level of *nirvana* realization is called an *Arhat*. An *Arhat*, through self-effort, has purged out all impurities, is full of wisdom and compassion, and after death will not be reborn.

The other major branch of Buddhism, the Mahayana, was shown to have focused on scriptural passages such as Buddha's silence in response to questions of a metaphysical nature (e.g. Is the world eternal or not?). In this tradition the status of the Buddha is raised from that of an ordinary man to one who has supra-human qualities: he is conceived without sexual intercourse, he is omniscient, and his death is a mere appearance. In reality he remains present in this world out of compassion for those who are still suffering. In line with this new image of the Buddha, the salvation goal for humans is not to become an *Arhat* but to become a *Bodhisattva* – one who vows not to go into *nirvana* until all other beings have realized release. In terms of philosophy, Mahayana thinkers, led by Nagarjuna (second century C.E.), criticized the Theravada theory of *dharmas* as the elements or parts that make up a person. Basing himself on the silence of the Buddha, Nagarjuna's approach was to show that all philosophical viewpoints whether Hindu or Theravada were ultimately hollow and obstructed one's realization of *nirvana*. As we saw in chapter 6, Nagarjuna's critique of viewpoints puts an end to all attempts to conceptualize reality through language, leaving only silent meditation as the path to release (as for example in Zen practice).

Over the years a critique developed of the idea that one had to become a monk or nun in order to realize *nirvana*. In the Theravada tradition of Ceylon and the Mahayana Jodo Shinshu tradition of Japan, ideas and practices developed that opened the way for laypeople who were married and holding down jobs to study, chant, and practice meditation in ways that could lead to release. Thus Buddhism, like Hinduism, came to offer a great variety of paths to salvation (*nirvana*) that serve monks, nuns, and laypeople alike.

We began this book with a quotation from T. S. Eliot's poem "Burnt Norton" and its image of "the still point" at the center of the turning world from which the pattern of the universe could be seen. In the above chapters, each world religion reviewed was seen to have its own vision of "the pattern of the universe" and of what we as humans must do to resonate with it. In answer to our childhood questions "Why am I here?" "What is the meaning of it all?" each religion provides its own answer. While the Jewish, Christian, and Muslim answers emphasize human sin and disobedience to God as the baseline of our human condition, the Eastern religions of Hinduism and Buddhism see the problem in terms of ignorance rather than sin, an ignorance which is self-caused by our free choices in this and previous lives. For Judaism, Christianity, and Islam, being saved from our sinfulness requires a mix of God's grace and human effort and promises a life after death in Heaven rather than Hell. By contrast, salvation for Hinduism and Buddhism is seen as release from a seemingly endless series of birth, death, and rebirth through the overcoming of ignorance. For Hinduism divine grace takes several forms or paths in helping devotees to realize *moksa*; in Buddhism more stress is placed on self-effort in the practice of compassion and meditation needed for the realization of *nirvana*. Through these various conceptions of sin and salvation each religious tradition offers its own vision of how we as individuals can participate in the pattern of the universe and so give our lives meaning. In these images, as Eliot put it, "past and future are gathered into the present."

Notes

CHAPTER 1

1. T. S. Eliot, "Burnt Norton," in *A Little Treasury of Modern Poetry*, ed. Oscar Williams (New York: Scribners, 1952), p. 29.
2. William James, *The Varieties of Religious Experience* (New York: Mentor, 1958).
3. See Henry S. Levinson, "Festive Naturalism and 'The Legends of the Jews,'" *Harvard Divinity Bulletin*, vol. 30, no. 2, 2001, p. 5.
4. Maurice Friedman, *A Heart of Wisdom: Religion and Human Wholeness* (Albany: State University of New York Press, 1992), p. 89.

CHAPTER 2

1. Jacob Neusner, *The Way of Torah: An Introduction to Judaism* (Belmont, CA: Dickenson Publishing Co., 1974), p. 12.
2. As quoted by Neusner, ibid., p. 13.
3. Ibid., p. 14.
4. Isidore Epstein, *Judaism* (New York: Penguin Books), 1987, p. 60.
5. Ibid., p. 61.
6. Anthony J. Saldarini and Joseph Kanofsky, "Religious Dimensions of the Human Condition in Judaism," in *The*

Human Condition, ed. Robert C. Neville (Albany: State University of New York Press, 2001), p. 104.

7. Ben Sirach 15:14–17 as quoted by Saldarini and Kanofsky, ibid., p. 108.

8. As quoted by Saldarini and Kanofsky, "Religious Dimensions," pp. 118–19.

9. Ibid., p. 102.

10. See "Redemption," in *Encyclopaedia Judaica*, vol. 14 (Jerusalem: Keter Publishing House, 1971), pp. 1–3.

11. Ephraim E. Urbach, *The Sages: Their Concepts and Beliefs*, trans. from the Hebrew by Israel Abrahams (Jerusalem: Magnes Press, 1975), Chapter XVII "On Redemption," pp. 649–92.

12. Ibid., p. 649.

13. *Encyclopaedia Judaica*, p. 3.

14. Ibid., p. 4.

15. Urbach, *Sages*, p. 657.

16. Ibid., p. 660.

17. Ibid., pp. 665–6.

18. Ibid., p. 667.

19. Ibid., p. 668.

20. Ibid., p. 669.

21. Ibid., p. 671.

22. Louis Finkelstein, *Akiba: Scholar, Saint and Martyr* (New York: Atheneum Books, 1970), p. 269.

23. Urbach, *Sages*, p. 673.

24. Ibid., p. 679.

25. Ibid.

26. Ibid., p. 683.

27. Ibid.

28. E. P. Saunders, *Paul and Palestinian Judaism* (Philadelphia: Fortress Press, 1977), p. 236.

29. *Encyclopaedia Judaica*, p. 4.

30. Ibid., pp. 4–5.

31. Ibid., p. 5. The following summary is from the *Judaica* article.

32. Ibid.

33. Ibid.

34. Ibid., pp. 5–6.

35. Ibid., p. 6.

36. Epstein, *Judaism*, p. 245.

37. *Encyclopaedia Judaica*, p. 6.
38. Epstein, *Judaism*, p. 245.
39. For more on this fascinating rebirth idea that bears some resonance with the Buddhist *Bodhisattva* (one who has realized enlightenment but stays behind to help others reach release rather than going off into *nirvana*) and the Hindu *rsi* (one who has reached release from rebirth in a previous life but is reborn at the start of each cycle of the universe to speak the Hindu scripture, the Veda, so as to help others obtain release), see Epstein, *Judaism*, pp. 246 ff.
40. Luria as summarized by Epstein, ibid., p. 246.
41. Ibid.
42. *Encyclopaedia Judaica*, p. 7.
43. Ibid.
44. Martin Buber, *I and Thou* (New York: Charles Scribners, 1958), p. 135.
45. Ibid., p. 11.
46. As quoted in *Encyclopaedia Judacia*, p. 7.
47. Ibid.
48. Ibid., p. 8.
49. As quoted in *Encyclopaedia Judaica*, p. 8.
50. Ibid.
51. Ibid., p. 9.
52. Ibid.
53. See Eliezer Segal, "Judaism," in *Life after Death in World Religions*, ed. Harold Coward (Maryknoll N.Y.: Orbis, 1997), p. 14.
54. Ibid., pp. 17–18.
55. Urbach, *Sages*, pp. 654ff.
56. Segal, "Judaism," pp. 18ff.
57. Ibid., p. 21.
58. "Ghenna," in *The Interpreter's Dictionary of the Bible*, vol. II (New York: Abingdon Press), 1962, p. 361.
59. Segal, "Judaism," p. 22.
60. Ibid., p. 24.
61. Ibid., p. 26.
62. Louis Jacobs, *Theology in Responsa* (London: Routledge & Kegan Paul, 1975), p. 260.

CHAPTER 3

1. Terence Penelhum, "Christianity," in *Life After Death in World Religions*, ed. Harold Coward (Maryknoll: Orbis Books, 2001), p. 31.
2. Ibid., p. 32.
3. Ibid., p. 33.
4. Ibid.
5. Paula Fredriksen, "Embodiment and Redemption: The Human Condition in Ancient Christianity," in *The Human Condition*, ed. Robert C. Neville (Albany: State University of New York Press, 2001), p. 135.
6. Karl Rahner, "Salvation: Theology," in *Sacramentum Mundi: An Encyclopedia of Theology*, vol. V (London: Burns & Oates, 1970), p. 426.
7. Willard G. Oxtoby, "Reflections on the idea of salvation," in *Man and his salvation*, ed. Eric Sharpe and John Hunnells (Manchester: Manchester University Press, 1973), p. 24.
8. T. B. Kilpatrick, "Salvation," in *Encyclopedia of Religion and Ethics*, ed. James Hastings, vol. XI (Edinburgh: T&T Clark, 1920), p. 120.
9. Peter Toon, "Salvation" in the *New Twentieth-Century Encyclopedia of Religious Knowledge*, ed. J. D. Douglas (Grand Rapids: Baker Book House, 1991), p. 732.
10. B. A. Gerrish, *Saving and Secular Faith* (Minneapolis: Fortress Press, 1989), p. 5.
11. Fredriksen, "Embodiment and Redemption," p. 135.
12. Ibid., p. 136.
13. Ibid., p. 137.
14. Ibid., p. 139.
15. *The New Encyclopedia Britannica*, vol. 8 (Chicago: Encyclopedia Britannica, 1989), p. 998.
16. Fredriksen, "Embodiment and Redemption," p. 141.
17. *The New Encyclopedia Britannica*, p. 998.
18. Saint Augustine, *The City of God*, ed. V. J. Bourke (New York: Doubleday & Co., 1958), "Introduction," p. 16.
19. *The New Encyclopedia Britannica*, vol. 25, p. 974.
20. Ibid.
21. *The City of God*, p. 318.
22. Ibid., p. 317.

23. Fredriksen, "Embodiment and Redemption," pp. 143–5.
24. Ibid., p. 144.
25. *The City of God*, pp. 540–5.
26. Fredriksen, "Embodiment and Redemption," p. 145.
27. Ibid.
28. B. A. Gerrish, *Saving the Secular Faith* (Minneapolis: Fortress Press, 1999), p. 6.
29. Ibid.
30. Ibid., p. 8.
31. *The New Encyclopedia Britannica*, vol. 23, p. 366.
32. As quoted by Gerrish, *Saving the Secular Faith*, p. 9.
33. Ibid.
34. Ibid., p. 10.
35. Ibid., p. 11.
36. John Calvin, *Institutes of the Christian Religion*, vol. 1, trans. Henry Beveridge (London: James Clarke & Co., 1962).
37. As quoted by Gerrish, *Saving the Secular Faith*, p. 12.
38. Ibid.
39. Ibid., p. 13.
40. *The New Encyclopedia Britannica*, vol. 26, p. 229.
41. Ibid., p. 230.
42. Friedrich Schleiermacher, *On Religion: Speeches to its Cultured Despisers*, trans. John Oman (New York: Harper & Row, 1958), p. 223.
43. Karl Barth, *The Word of God and the Word of Man*, trans. Douglas Horton (London: Hodder & Stroughton, 1928), p. 227.
44. Gerrish, *Saving the Secular Faith*, p. 56.
45. Ibid., p. 84.
46. As paraphrased by Gerrish, ibid., p. 86.
47. George Tavard, *Holy Writ or Holy Church* (London: Burns & Oates, 1959), p. 209.
48. Wolfgang Beinert and Francis Schussler Fiorenza, eds., *Handbook of Catholic Theology* (New York: Crossroad, 1945), p. 641.
49. "Eastern Orthodoxy," in *The New Encyclopedia Britannica*, vol. 17, p. 878.
50. Ibid.
51. Penelhum, "Christianity," p. 41.
52. Paul W. Gooch, *Partial Knowledge* (Notre Dame: University of Notre Dame Press, 1987), chap. 3.

53. Oscar Cullman, "Immortality of the Soul or Resurrection of the Dead," in *Immortality*, ed. Terence Penelhum (Belmont: Wadsworth, 1973), p. 73.
54. Ibid.
55. Sallie McFague, *The Body of God: An Ecological Theology* (Minneapolis: Fortress Press, 1993).
56. Lucy Tatman, "Salvation," in *An A to Z of Feminist Theology*, ed. Lisa Isherwood and Dorothea McEwan (Sheffield: Sheffield Academic Press, 1996), p. 213.
57. Ibid.

CHAPTER 4

1. Hanna E. Kassis, *A Concordance of the Qur'an*, Foreword by Fazlur Rahman (Berkeley: University of California Press, 1983), p. 837.
2. As quoted by Frederick Denny in "Salvation in the Qur'an," in *In Quest of an Islamic Humanism*, ed. A. H. Green (Cairo: The American University in Cairo Press, 1984), p. 206.
3. Muhammad Abul Quasem, *Salvation of the Soul and Islamic Devotions* (London: Kegan Paul, 1981), p. 19.
4. S. Nomanul Haq, "The Human Condition in Islam," in *The Human Condition*, ed. Robert Neville (Albany: State University of New York Press, 2001), p. 171.
5. Ibid.
6. Translated by Hanna Kassis in his chapter "The Qur'an," in *Experiencing Scripture in World Religions*, ed. Harold Coward (Maryknoll, N.Y.: Orbis Books, 2000), p. 69.
7. Frederick M. Denny, "The Problem of Salvation in the Quran: Key Terms and Concepts," in *In Quest of an Islamic Humanism*, ed. A. H. Green, p. 197.
8. James Robson, "Aspects of the Qur'anic doctrine of salvation," in *Man and his salvation*, ed. Eric Sharpe and John Hinnells (Manchester: Manchester University Press, 1973), p. 206.
9. Ibid.
10. John Renard, "Deliverance," in *Encyclopaedia of the Qur'an*, ed. Jane Dammen McAuliffe (Leiden: Brill, 2001), p. 319.
11. As quoted by Jeremy Hinds, "Salvation," in *Encyclopaedia of the Holy Qur'an*, ed. N. K. Singh and A. R. Agwan (Delhi: Global Vision Publishing House, 2000), pp. 1322–3.

12. Renard, "Deliverance," p. 519.
13. W. R. W. Gardner, *The Qur'anic Doctrine of Salvation* (London: The Christian Literature Society for India, 1914), pp. 7–11.
14. Denny, "The Problem of Salvation," p. 198.
15. Robson, "Aspects of the Qur'anic doctrine of salvation," p. 205.
16. As quoted by Denny, "The Problem of Salvation," p. 207.
17. Robson, "Aspects of the Qur'anic doctrine of salvation," p. 205.
18. Ibid., p. 206.
19. As quoted by Rolland Miller, "The Muslim Doctrine of Salvation," *Bulletin of Christian Institutes of Islamic Studies*, vol. 3, nos. 1–4, 1980, p. 145.
20. Denny, "The Problem of Salvation," p. 206.
21. Ibid.
22. Ibid.
23. As quoted by Denny, "The Problem of Salvation," p. 199.
24. Ibid., p. 200.
25. Fazlur Rahman, *Major Themes of the Qur'an* (Minneapolis: Bibliotheca Islamica, 1980), p. 69.
26. As quoted by Denny, "The Problem of Salvation," p. 201.
27. Ibid.
28. Robson, "Aspects of the Qur'anic doctrine of salvation," p. 215.
29. As quoted by Robson, ibid.
30. Ibid., p. 216.
31. Denny, "The Problem of Salvation," p. 203.
32. Ibid.
33. *The Holy Qur'an: English Translation of the Meanings and Commentary* (Saudi Arabia: King Fahd Holy Qur'an Printing Complex, A.H. 1411), p. 1940.
34. Rahman, "*Major Themes*," p. 63.
35. Denny, "The Problem of Salvation," p. 63.
36. Ibid.
37. Robson, "Aspects of the Qur'anic doctrine of salvation," pp. 206–7.
38. Ibid., p. 219.
39. Rolland Miller, "The Muslim Doctrine of Salvation," *Bulletin of Christian Institutes of Islamic Studies*, vol. 3, nos. 1–4,

1980, p. 146. What follows is based mainly on Miller's analysis of "The Means of Salvation," pp. 145–88. Miller bases his approach on Quasem, *Salvation of the Soul*.

40. Ibid., p. 147.
41. As quoted by Miller, "The Muslim Doctrine of Salvation," p. 149.
42. Ibid., p. 150.
43. Ibid., p. 151.
44. As quoted by Miller, ibid.
45. As quoted by Miller, ibid., p. 153.
46. Ibid., p. 154.
47. Ibid., p. 153.
48. As quoted by Miller, *Muslim Friends: Their Faith and Feeling* (St. Louis: Concordia Publishing House, 1995), p. 201.
49. Ibid., p. 202.
50. As quoted by Miller, "The Muslim Doctrine of Salvation," p. 162.
51. Ibid.
52. As quoted by Miller in *Muslim Friends*, p. 202.
53. Miller, "The Muslim Doctrine of Salvation," p. 165.
54. Ibid., p. 166.
55. As quoted by Miller, ibid.
56. As quoted by Miller, ibid., p. 167.
57. Ibid., p. 169.
58. Miller, *Muslim Friends*, p. 202.
59. As quoted by Miller, "The Muslim Doctrine of Salvation," p. 171.
60. Ibid., p. 173.
61. Ibid., pp. 174–5.
62. As quoted by Miller, ibid., p. 174.
63. Ibid.
64. Ibid., p. 175.
65. Ibid., p. 176.
66. Muhammad Abul Quasem, *Salvation of the Soul*, p. 35.
67. Ibid.
68. Ibid.
69. Miller, "The Muslim Doctrine of Salvation," p. 180.
70. Ibid., p. 181.
71. As quoted by Miller, ibid.
72. Ibid., p. 182.

73. Ibid., p. 184.
74. As quoted by Miller, ibid., pp. 185–6.
75. *Muslim Friends*, p. 204.
76. As quoted by Miller, ibid.
77. Annemarie Schimmel, "A 'sincere Muhammahan's way to salvation'," in *Man and his Salvation*, ed. Eric Sharpe and John Hinnells (Manchester: Manchester University Press, 1973), pp. 221–42.
78. Ibid., p. 225.
79. Ibid., pp. 226–7.
80. Ibid., p. 231.
81. Ibid., pp. 232–3.
82. See pp. 233–42 of Schimmel's treatment of Dard's experience of "Light."
83. Ibid., p. 242.
84. Miller, *Muslim Friends*, p. 205.
85. Hanna Kassis, "Islam," in *Life After Death in World Religions*, ed. Harold Coward (Maryknoll: Orbis Books, 2000), p. 52.
86. This description is taken from Kassis, ibid., pp. 52–4.
87. Ibid., p. 55.
88. Ibid., p. 58.
89. As quoted by Kassis, ibid., p. 59.
90. Ibid.
91. Miller, *Muslim Friends*, p. 205.
92. As quoted by Kassis, "Islam," p. 60.
93. Miller, *Muslim Friends*, p. 206.
94. As quoted by Kassis, "Islam," p. 61.
95. Miller, *Muslim Friends*, p. 207.

CHAPTER 5

1. As translated by Robert Ernest Hume, *The Thirteen Principal Upanisads* (Oxford: Oxford University Press, 1968), p. 80.
2. As cited by Troy W. Organ, *The Hindu Quest for the Perfection of Man* (Athens, Ohio: Ohio University, 1970), p. 5.
3. Ibid.
4. The following explanation of *karma* is taken from the *Yoga Sutras* of Patanjali, *Sutras* II:12–14 and IV:7–9. For an English translation see *The Yoga System of Patanjali*, trans. J. H.

Woods, Harvard Oriental Series, vol. 17 (Varanasi: Motilal Banarsidass, 1966). For a detailed analysis of the passages in question see Harold G. Coward, "Psychology and Karma," *Philosophy East and West*, 33, 1983, pp. 49–60. There are many definitions of *karma* in Hindu thought, some making *karma* appear quite deterministic. The *Yoga Sutra* definition is presented here because it is clearly formulated and is widely accepted by scholars within the tradition.

5. Harold Coward, *Scripture in the World Religions: A Short Introduction* (Oxford: Oneworld, 2000).
6. Aurobindo Ghose, *The Secret of the Veda* (Pondicherry: Sri Aurobindo Ashram, 1971), p. 8.
7. The dating of the various layers of Hindu scripture varies from scholar to scholar, and is at best speculative. The dates given are taken mainly from David Kinsley, *Hinduism* (Englewood Cliffs, N. J.: Prentice-Hall, 1982), p. 12.
8. *Chandogya Upanisad* 7.25.2, trans. Hume, *The Thirteen Principal Upanisads*, p. 261.
9. *Isa Upanisad*, v. 9, trans. S. Radhadrishnan, *The Principal Upanisads* (London: George Allen & Unwin, 1968), p. 573.
10. *Mundaka Upanisad* 3.2.3, trans. Radhakrishnan.
11. Ibid., 3.1.9.
12. Ibid., 3.2.1.
13. *Chandogya Upanisad* 8.4.2, trans. Hume.
14. *Maitri Upanisad* 4.4, trans. Radhakrishnan.
15. *Brhad-Aranyaka Upanisad* 5.14.8, trans. Hume.
16. Ibid., 4.3–4.
17. Ibid., 4.3.6.
18. Other *Mahavakayas* or "great summary sentences" of the *Upanisads* include: *aham Brahma asmi* or "I am *Brahman*;" *ayam atma Brahma* or "This *Atman* is *Brahman*;" and *prajnanam Brahma* or "Consciousness is *Brahman*."
19. *The Bhagavad Gita*, trans. R. C. Zaehner (Oxford: Oxford University Press, 1969), 2.47, p. 145.
20. *The Bhagavad Gita*, trans. Barbara Stoler Miller (New York: Bantam, 1986), 12:6–8, p. 112.
21. For example, see Zaehner's translation and commentary.
22. As translated by Zaehner, 2:39.
23. For a readable English translation see *Patanjali's Yoga Sutras*, trans. Rama Prasada (New Delhi: Oriental Books, 1978).

24. *The Brahma Sutra*, trans. S. Radhakrishnan (London: Allen & Unwin, 1960).
25. *Brahma-Sutra Bhasya of Sankaracarya*, trans. Swami Gambhirananda (Calcutta: Advaita Ashrama, 1977).
26. See *Advaita Vedanta Up to Sankara and His Pupils*, ed. Karl Potter (Princeton: Princeton University Press, 1981).
27. For excerpts of Vivekananda's talks in Europe and North America see *Sources of Indian Tradition*, vol. 2, ed. Stephen Hay (New York: Columbia University Press, 1988), pp. 72ff.
28. Anantanand Rambachan, *The Limits of Scripture: Vivekananda's Reinterpretation of the Vedas* (Honolulu: University of Hawaii Press, 1994).
29. Ibid., pp. 5–6.
30. R. Balasubramanian, "Two Contemporary Exemplars of the Hindu Tradition: Ramana Maharsi and Sri Candrasekharendra Sarasvati," in *Hindu Spirituality: Vedas Through Vedanta*, ed. Krishna Sivaraman (New York: Crossroad, 1989), pp. 361–91.
31. Ibid., p. 364.
32. *Brhad-Aranyaka Upanisad* 2.4.5.
33. As quoted by Balasubramanian, "Two Contemporary Exemplars," p. 366.
34. Ibid., p. 372. Other scholars (e.g. Anatanand Rambachan) challenge this interpretation by arguing that it is not the world but ignorance (*avidya*) that disappears.
35. Ibid., p. 374.
36. The following presentation of the Srivaisnava tradition is based largely on Vasudha Narayanan, "*Karma, Bhaktiyoga* and Grace in the Srivaisnava Tradition: Ramaniya and Karattabvan," in *Of Human Bondage and Divine Grace*, ed. John Carter (La Salle, IL. Open Court, 1992), pp. 57–94.
37. Ibid., p. 58.
38. Ibid., p. 60.
39. Ibid., pp. 60–1.
40. Ibid., p. 62.
41. Ramanuja's Commentary on the *Bhagavad Gita* 10:10 and 11 and 13:6 and 7 as quoted by Narayanan, "*Karma, Bhaktiyoga* and Grace," p. 63.
42. Ibid., p. 69.

43. Vasudha Narayanan, "Bondage and Grace in the Srivaisanava Tradition: Pilai Lokacharya and Vedanta Desika," in *Of Human Bondage and Divine Grace*, ed. John Carter, p. 83.

44. Robert Baird, "Swami Bhaktivedanta and Ultimacy" in *Religion in Modern India*, ed. Robert Baird (Delhi: Manohar, 1995), p. 516.

45. As quoted by Baird, ibid., p. 522.

46. Ibid., p. 527.

47. Trans. Barbara Stoler Miller, p. 36.

48. *Bhagavad Gita* 2:42–69.

49. *The Gitabhasya of Ramanuja*, trans. M. R. Sampatkumaran (Madras: Ramacharya Memorial Trust, 1969), p. 55.

50. *Jnaneshwar's Gita*, trans. Swami Kripananda (Albany: State University of New York Press, 1989), p. 34.

51. M. K. Gandhi, *The Bhagavadaita* (Delhi: Orient, n.d.), p. 14.

52. See Harold Coward, "Ambedkar, Gandhi and the Untouchables," in *Indian Critiques of Gandhi*, ed. Harold Coward (Albany: State University of New York Press, 2003).

53. Organ, *The Hindu Quest*, p. 239.

54. As quoted by Organ, ibid., p. 246.

55. Perhaps the most readable translation is by Rama Prasada, *Patanjali's Yoga Sutras* (Delhi: Oriental Books, 1978). A more recent translation is by Jean Varenne, *Yoga and the Hindu Tradition* (Delhi: Motilal Banarsidass, 1989).

56. See Gerald Larson, *Classical Sankhya* (Delhi: Motilal Banarsidass, 1979).

57. Aurobindo Ghose, *On the Veda* (Pondicherry: Sri Aurobindo Ashram Press, 1956). For a good overall study of Aurobindo see Robert Munor, *Sri Aurobindo: The Perfect and the Good* (Calcutta: Minerva, 1978). The *ashram* that Aurobindo created is critically examined by Robert Minor, *The Religious, the Spiritual and the Secular: Auroville and Secular India* (Albany: State University of New York Press, 1999).

58. As quoted by Sisirkumar Ghose, "Sri Aurobindo: The Spirituality of the Future," in *Hindu Spirituality: Postclassical and Modern*, ed. K. R. Sundararajan and Bithika Mukerji (New York: Crossroads, 1997), p. 387.

CHAPTER 6

1. From the Buddhist scriptures, *The Tripitaka*, as quoted by J. Perez-Remon, "Liberation in Early Buddhism," in *Salvation in Christianity and Other Religions* (Rome: Gregorian University Press, 1980), p. 167.
2. Walpola Rahula, *What the Buddha Taught* (New York: Grove Press, 1974 and Oxford: Oneworld, 1977), p. 1.
3. As quoted by Rahula, ibid., p. 3.
4. Ibid., p. 3.
5. The following is based on Rahula, ibid., pp. 19ff.
6. Alex Wayman, "Buddha as Saviour," in *Salvation in Christianity and Other Religions*, no editor given (Rome: Gregorian University Press, 1980), p. 196.
7. Yun-Hua Jan, "Dimensions of Indian Buddhism," in *The Malalasekera Commemoration Volume*, ed. O. H. de A. Wijesekera (Colombo, Sri Lanka: 1976), p. 162.
8. The following is based upon K. N. Jayatilleke, *Early Buddhist Theory of Knowledge* (Delhi: Motilal Banarsidass, 1980), pp. 183ff.
9. Lewis Lancaster, "Buddhist Literature: Its Canons, Scribes and Editors," in *The Critical Study of Sacred Texts*, ed. Wendy Doniger O'Flaherty (Berkeley: Berkeley Religious Studies Series, 1979), p. 216.
10. As quoted by Malcolm David Eckel, "Beginningless Ignorance," in *The Human Condition*, ed. R. C. Neville (Albany: State University of New York Press, 2001), pp. 50–1.
11. Richard Robinson, *The Buddhist Religion* (Belmont, CA.: Dickenson, 1970), p. 28.
12. L. Schmithausen, "On Some Aspects of Descriptions or Theories of 'Liberating Insight' and 'Enlightenment' in Early Buddhism," *Studien Zum Jainismus und Buddhismus*, 23, 1983, pp. 200–1.
13. Robinson, *The Buddhist Religion*, p. 19.
14. Ibid., p. 31.
15. As quoted by Richard Gombrich, *Theravada Buddhism: A Social History from Ancient Benares to Modern Colombo* (London: Routledge & Kegan Paul, 1988), p. 67.
16. Ibid.

17. Damien Keown, *Buddhism: A Very Short Introduction* (Oxford: Oxford University Press, 1996), p. 47.
18. Ibid.
19. See N. R. Reat, *Buddhism: A History* (Berkeley: Asian Humanities Press, 1994), p. 37.
20. For a clear presentation of the theory of "dependent arising" see Hirakawa Akira, *A History of Indian Buddhism*, trans. Paul Groner (Honolulu: University of Hawaii Press, 1990), pp. 51ff.
21. Ibid., p. 53.
22. Rahula, *What the Buddha Taught*, p. 8.
23. Gombrich, *Theravada Buddhism*, p. 73.
24. Akira, *History of Indian Buddhism*, p. 62.
25. The above listing of rules is taken from Akira, ibid., pp. 62–6.
26. Gombrich, *Theravada Buddhism*, pp. 172ff.
27. Ibid., p. 187.
28. Ibid., p. 191.
29. Ibid., p. 199.
30. T. R. V. Murti, *The Central Philosophy of Buddhism* (London: Allen & Unwin, 1960), p. 77.
31. Ibid.
32. The following outline of the origins of Mahayana Buddhism is based on Paul Williams, *Mahayana Buddhism: The Doctrinal Foundations* (London: Routledge, 1989), pp. 16ff.
33. Ibid., p. 19.
34. Ibid., p. 20.
35. Ibid., p. 33.
36. Ibid., p. 37.
37. Edward Conze, *Selected Sayings from the Perfection of Wisdom* (London: Buddhist Society, 1968), pp. 11ff.
38. Williams, *Mahayana Buddhism*, p. 49.
39. *L'Abhidharmakossa de Vasubandu*, trans. Louis de la Vallee Poussin (Paris: Paul Geuthner, 1923–35), vol. 6, p. 139.
40. Jeffrey R. Timm, "Prolegomena to Vallabha's Theology of Revelation," *Philosophy East and West*, vol. 38, no. 2, 1988, p. 109.
41. See Mervyn Sprung, *Lucid Exposition of the Middle Way* (London: Routledge & Kegan Paul, 1979). This deconstructive approach is nicely exemplified in the analysis of the statement, "the human soul is eternal" offered by Nagarjuna

and his commentator Candrakirti. Candrakirti asks what is the relationship between the subject "the human soul" and the predication "is eternal"; are the two terms identical or different? If the two terms are identical, we are left with a tautology: the eternal human soul is eternal. If they are different and distinct what could possibly justify the claim that they are related? See Timm, "Prolegomena," p. 109, and *Lucid Exposition of the Middle Way*, pp. 165–86.

42. Gadjin M. Nagoa, "From Madhyamika to Yogacara: An Analysis of MMK XXIV.18 and MV 1.1–2," *Journal of the International Association of Buddhist Studies*, 2, 1979, p. 32.

43. Richard H. Robinson, *Early Madhamika in India and China* (Delhi: Motilal Banarsidass, 1978), p. 49.

44. See the discussion of *nirvana*, ibid., pp. 46–7.

45. David Loy, "How Not to Criticize Nagarjuna: A Response to L. Stafford Betty." *Philosophy East and West*, vol. 34, no. 4, 1984, p. 443.

46. Private correspondence from David Loy, September 29, 1989.

47. Williams, *Mahayana Buddhism*, chaps 3–9.

48. Keown, *Buddhism*, p. 67.

49. *The New Encyclopedia Britannica* (Chicago: Encyclopedia Britannica, 1989), vol. 15, p. 303.

50. Williams, *Mahayana Buddhism*, p. 227.

51. For an illustration of how this "Pure Land" practice has adapted to a Canadian setting see David Goa and Harold Coward, "Sacred Ritual, Sacred Language: Jodo Shinshu Religious Forms in Transition," *Studies in Religion*, vol. 12, no. 4, 1983, pp. 363–79.

52. Williams, *Mahayana Buddhism*, p. 227.

Index